Sharing in Christ's Victory over Death

SHARING IN CHRIST'S VICTORY OVER DEATH

LIVING YOUR LIFE IN THE LIGHT OF ETERNITY

DEREK PRINCE

SHARING IN CHRIST'S VICTORY OVER DEATH
Living Your Life in the Light of Eternity

This book was previously published under the title 'The End of Life's Journey'

Unless otherwise specified, all Scriptures are taken from The Holy Bible, New King James Version © 1979, 1980, 1982 by Thomas Nelson, Inc., Nashville, Tennessee.

Scripture references marked NIV are taken from The Holy Bible, New International Version copyright © 1978 by New York International Bible Society.

Scripture references marked NASB are taken from New American Standard Bible, © 1960, 1962, 1963, 1971, 1973 by The Lockman Foundation.

ISBN 978-1-78263-494-2
ePub 978-1-78263-496-6
Kindle 978-1-78263-495-9
Product code: B62EN3

© 2004 Derek Prince Ministries – International

Taken from transcripts of the following messages: "Victory Over Death" (015–017), "Resurrection" (108–109), "The Resurrection" (4429).

Derek Prince Ministries www.derekprince.com

Set in Arno Pro by Raphaël Freeman, Renana Typesetting
Cover design by Guiding Productions

Table of Contents

Foreword

I was asked to write the foreword to this book three months after my beloved husband Jim had died. I was feeling overwhelmed with grief, sadness and the loss of the one with whom I had spent forty-three happy and fulfilled years.

I started reading 'Sharing in Christ's Victory over Death' and found many answers to questions that had been going through my mind, as well as help and comfort from the Scriptures that Daddy had used.

I had been brought up in a Christian home and thought I knew what happens to our loved ones when they die. But when I was confronted by my own tragedy, I was surprised and dismayed that I was unable to see things clearly from Scripture. The manuscript arrived at just the right time and I found reading it brought me real hope: I was not alone, God was with me in my grief and sorrow and He comforted me.

I pray this book will also be a blessing to those who are overwhelmed with grief and need help and encouragement in their time of loss. God bless you.

Kirsten Fry, daughter of Lydia and Derek Prince
23 November 2004

1

DEATH: THE UNIVERSAL APPOINTMENT

Is there something in you that flinches just for a moment at the mention of the word death? Is your first reaction to lay this book aside? If so, that is a sure indication that you, in particular, need to open your heart to this message.

In our contemporary culture, there has been an unadvertised effort to remove anything that might be unpleasant or painful from the concept of death. For instance, there have been subtle changes in terminology. We no longer speak about a funeral home, instead we use phrases such as "a parlor of rest" or perhaps "a chapel of rest." We no longer speak about a cemetery, instead we use a phrase such as "a memorial garden." And when the body of a dead person is displayed for view before burial, everything possible is done to minimize the changes caused by death.

I have heard psychological arguments advanced on behalf of these changes, and I am not interested in contesting these arguments. I am concerned, however, that we do not allow ourselves to forget one simple, objective, unchanging fact: death is real and it is unpleasant. It is painful and cruel. Any view of life that cannot accept this fact is deceptive and unrealistic. Any philosophy or religion that does not have a positive answer to the reality of death is inadequate to meet the needs of humanity. What distinguishes the Christian faith from all other religions and philosophies is that it has a positive, proven answer to death.

My basis for approaching this subject is threefold: through Scripture, personal experience and personal observation. First we will look at Scripture. In 1 Corinthians 15:26, Paul says, "The last enemy...is death." Death is an enemy, the universal enemy of the whole human race.

Then I want to say something from my own personal experience. Being nearly 90 years of age, I have, of course, experienced the loss of close relatives and loved ones: father, mother, and grandparents, to name a few. But most of all, I lost my two beloved wives, Lydia and then Ruth. With Lydia I had shared many years of happy marriage. More recently, God called Ruth home, which was a very hard experience for me. But God has brought me through in victory by His grace. And I am rejoicing in the fact that there is a resurrection.

Sometimes I look at married couples enjoying each other and I realize that sooner or later one of them is going to go. That is why I am so concerned to impart this truth to you so that when the time comes you will be victorious. Personally, God has given me the victory. It is a gift, and certainly not the result of my righteousness.

I believe in the resurrection! You see, I have two wives waiting for me on the other side! I did not marry them both at the same time, I want you to know, but one after the other. I lived with Lydia for thirty years and with Ruth for twenty years, so altogether, I was married for fifty years. And the wonderful part is I am going to see them both again!

From personal observation, I can tell you that during World War II I served as a hospital attendant in the battlefields and in the hospitals of North Africa. I encountered death many times. Also, as a minister, there were occasions when I was called in for counseling and helping the bereaved. So I am not speaking merely from theory or from ministerial training, but from the realities of life as I have lived it and seen it.

REACTIONS TO DEATH

Over the centuries man's reaction to death has taken various forms. One response is *cynicism*. This is expressed in a passage in Isaiah, which is a picture of men faced with the reality of imminent death:

> But instead, joy and gladness,
> Slaying oxen and killing sheep,
> Eating meat and drinking wine:
> "Let us eat and drink, for tomorrow we die."
>
> Isaiah 22:13

That is the cynical way to look at things: eat and drink, for death is soon coming.

Another reaction is pessimism. This was common in medieval Europe. The whole of medieval society was prevailed by a sense of death. It occurred in all their letters, their religion, their books, and even in their art.

Another reaction is what I would call morbid preoccupation. This attitude is described by the British poet, T.S. Eliot. Writing about a poet of the Elizabethan period in England named Webster, Eliot says this:

Webster was much possessed with death;
    He saw the skull beneath the skin,
And breastless creatures underground
    Leaned backwards with a lipless grin.

This depicts a man whose mind was totally occupied by death.

Another attitude is *escapism*. This is really the attitude of many Oriental cults and philosophies that are claiming our attention today. They speak about aiming at the release of the individual from his personal being into a kind of vague, non-personal existence called "nirvana." However, this is unreal. It is also contrary to Scripture. As a younger man, I myself was in that kind of cult for quite awhile, and I found in it nothing but frustration – certainly not fulfillment.

Let us turn now to the faithful record of Scripture and see what it has to say. Hebrews 9:27 tells it like it is: "And as it is appointed for men to die once, but after this the judgment." Somebody has said, "You may miss every appointment you ever made while you live, but there are two appointments you're going to keep: the first is death, the second is judgment."

Someone once commented concerning the resurrection of Jesus: *Jesus is the only Person who made an appointment beyond the grave and kept it.* He is unique in that way – and many other ways too. And because He was resurrected, all those who believe in Him and follow Him will also be resurrected. We will be called forth from the grave.

ACCOUNTABILITY

The Bible clearly reveals (and we will see this in greater detail later) that there is continuing conscious existence after death and also personal accountability for what we have done during our lives.

Accountability is a word that is not popular today in contemporary culture. People attempt to banish it from their minds. There is an attempt to run from it. But the fact remains that it is appointed for men to die once and after this comes judgment. We will be held accountable.

When modern medicine encounters a physical problem it seeks to provide three things: diagnosis, prognosis, and remedy. The diagnosis reveals the cause; the prognosis predicts the course that the disease will take; and the remedy, of course, is the answer to the disease.

When we face the topic of death, the Bible offers us all three of these things: diagnosis, prognosis and remedy. First, there is the diagnosis – the cause. This is stated very simply in Scripture: "Therefore, just as through one man sin entered the world, and death through sin, and thus death spread to all men, because all sinned…" (Romans 5:12).

So, death came through sin. If there had never been sin, there never would have been death. But because all men have sinned, death comes to all men.

Again, in 1 Corinthians 15:56, Paul says, "The sting of death is sin." We all know what a sting is. It is the means by which some kind of insect injects its poison into the body of its victim and thereby produces a negative result. The means by which death injected its corruption into our bodies was sin. Sin is the sting that injects the poison of death.

Second, we have the prognosis. The Bible indicates that death comes in three successive stages. The first is spiritual death. God said to Adam, as He warned him about the tree of knowledge of good and evil: "…but of the tree of the knowledge of good and evil you shall not eat, for in the day that you eat of it you shall surely die" (Genesis 2:17).

God told Adam *"in the day that you eat* you will die." As we understand death, Adam lived another 900 years and more. But in the very day that he sinned he was cut off, or alienated from, a life with God. In that moment he died spiritually. In Ephesians 2:1 Paul reminds the Christians in Ephesus what their spiritual condition was before they knew Christ: "And you *He made alive,* who were *dead* in trespasses and sins ..." (*emphasis added*).

Paul was not speaking of a physical death, but a spiritual death – alienation from God. Once man's spirit was cut off from God by sin, his physical life was like a battery that could not be recharged. It continued to function for quite a while, but ultimately it would run down.

The second phase is physical death. This is what we actually call "death" – the separation of the soul from the body. There is a visible result in the condition of the body. It begins to decay. But the condition of the soul remains unchanged.

The third phase is what the Bible calls "the second death." This is something that is known only through the revelation of Scripture: "This is the second death. And anyone not found written in the Book of Life was cast into the lake of fire" (Revelation 20:14–15).

As we study the picture presented here in Revelation, we see two important things. First, this second death is final, eternal, irrevocable banishment from the presence of God. From the second death there is no way back. Second, it is not a cessation of consciousness, for there is never a cessation of consciousness. Personality remains conscious both in this life and in the world beyond, forever and ever. We never escape from our own consciousness.

Let me briefly review the three phases of the Bible's prognosis of the course of death in human life:

1. Spiritual death – the alienation of man's soul from God through sin.
2. Physical death – the separation of the soul from the body.
3. The "second death" – the final, irrevocable banishment from the presence of God but yet with continuing consciousness.

In the following chapters, I will go on to present the Bible's remedy for death.

2

THE LIFE-GIVER
AND THE LIFE-TAKER

It is only after we have accepted both the diagnosis and prognosis that we can begin to understand and apply the remedy.

In order to do this, I must first explain more fully the nature of the spiritual world and the spiritual forces that are at work both in life and in death. Some people do not realize that there is a spiritual world. They think everything begins and ends in this world and that there is nothing beyond. Other people acknowledge the reality of a spiritual world, but they think of it as something vague, amorphous or abstract. But the truth is that the spiritual world is as real and objective as the physical world, and it is occupied with both things and persons more numerous and varied than all that we are familiar with in the physical world. The really important difference between the two worlds is that the physical is temporary and transient and the spiritual is eternal and unchanging. In 2 Corinthians 4:18, Paul expresses it this way: "...we do not look at the things which are seen, but at the things which are not seen. For the things which are seen are temporary, but the things which are not seen are eternal."

Two Persons

From this we see that the unseen world is eternal. Let us now explore what the Bible shows us about the nature of this unseen world. If we trace life and death back to their sources, we come face to face with two persons whom I have entitled the *life-giver* and the *life-taker*. In John 10:10 this is expressed very clearly in the words of Jesus: "The thief does not come except to steal, and to kill, and to destroy. I have come that they may have life, and that they may have it more abundantly."

There we have the two persons: the thief and Jesus. Each of them is equally a person. The name of the thief, of course, is Satan. So many people today find it difficult to realize that Satan is a real person. I read something in a book once that really gripped me. It said, "Evil is not some*thing*, but some*one*." When we realize that, our eyes are beginning to be opened. So the thief is Satan or the devil. Certainly Jesus spoke the truth with tremendous frankness when disclosing the nature of our enemy, the devil. He said to the religious people of His day:

> You are of your father the devil, and the desires of your father you want to do. He was a murderer from the beginning, and does not stand in the truth, because there is no truth in him. When he speaks a lie, he speaks from his own resources, for he is a liar and the father of it.
>
> John 8:44

So Jesus tells us that Satan (the devil) is a liar and a murderer. Put that together with the passage in John 10:10, and we find out that Satan is a thief, a liar, and a murderer. The Bible has nothing good to tell us about him.

A well-known evangelist once summed up the difference

between God and the devil in this simple phrase: "There is no badness in God, and there is no goodness in the devil." We need to bear that in mind. We do not want to be blinded by philosophy or sentimentality or human theory. We are dealing with two persons: the life-giver, who is Jesus; and the life-taker, Satan, the devil.

We need to always keep in mind John 10:10, where Jesus said: "The thief does not come except to steal, and to kill, and to destroy." The devil never comes into our life to do us good. He has three purposes, and each is worse than the one before. His first purpose is to steal, his second to kill, his third to destroy.

Satan's destructive work against us does not end with physical death but continues on into eternity. He is a murderer, a thief, and a liar. The fact that he is a thief and a liar should warn us of one thing: he is out to deceive us. When he comes to us, he does not tell us who he is or the purpose for which he comes. Ordinarily, a thief does not walk up to your house, knock on your door, and when you open say, "I'm a thief. I have come to take your possessions." More often, he comes in the dark, at a time when you cannot see him and you do not expect him. Or, a different kind of thief is a con man. He will come and misrepresent his motive, suggesting to you that he has something tremendously valuable to impart to you, but really he has come to take and not to give.

God *is* light; He works in the light. When we are related to God, we can know to whom we are related. We can be aware of what God is doing. We do not need to grope or to fumble. We are not uncertain or insecure. But the devil, Satan, works in the dark. Often when he is at work, we do not see him or recognize him. We do not know exactly who he is or why he is there or what he is doing. When God is in our lives, we recognize Him.

But when Satan is in our lives, many times we fail to recognize him. He is a deceiver and a liar.

Once, when I was the principal of a college in Africa for training teachers, one of the African teachers under me had tremendous problems about the reality of the devil. At the time, he had a small flock of ducks that he was caring for in his back yard. He was very proud of his ducks. One day he came to me so forlorn and disappointed because someone had come in the night and stolen all his ducks. I said to him, "Mr. Odawa, did that person come to your door and tell you that he was coming to steal your ducks?"

He said, "No. No, he came in the dark and I didn't see him."

I said, "Mr. Odawa, that explains your problem with the reality of the devil. He doesn't come to the door in the light and knock and say, 'I'm the devil. I have come to steal.' But he does just like that thief who took your ducks. He comes in the night. He doesn't tell you who he is or when he is coming. You don't see him or you don't recognize him, and you don't know what you are dealing with. That is the way a thief works."

Remember that Jesus said that the devil is a thief, a liar, and a murderer. He never comes to do us any good. He has three purposes: to steal all the blessings God wants us to enjoy; to kill by taking our physical lives; and to destroy by tormenting us forever and ever in a lost eternity.

Thank God for Jesus, who is so faithful to tell us the truth! Thank God also that Jesus is the remedy, as we will see in the next chapter.

3

THE KINSMAN-REDEEMER

We cannot talk about the remedy for death without looking at the Bible's picture of Jesus as our kinsman-redeemer. This is one of the most vivid and beautiful pictures of Him found in the Old Testament. We will begin by looking at the purpose for which Jesus came: "For this purpose the Son of God was manifested, that He might destroy the works of the devil" (1 John 3:8).

What were the works of the devil? We saw in the last chapter that the devil comes to steal, to kill, and to destroy. The Son of God, on the other hand, came to undo everything that the devil had done against us. We need a clear vision of these two persons: Jesus, the life-giver; and Satan, the life-taker.

In order to fulfill the purpose for which He came, Jesus had to identify Himself with us, that is, with the human race. One of the favorite titles that He used of Himself, almost more than any other in the Gospels, was "Son of Man," or "Son of Adam" – a descendant of Adam, a member of the human race. This is plainly stated in Hebrews 2:14: "Since the children have flesh and blood, he too [Jesus] shared in their humanity so that by his death he might destroy him who holds the power of death – that is, the devil…" (NIV).

Notice again the clear delineation of persons and responsibilities. The one who holds the power of death is the devil. Jesus came to defeat him, to destroy him, and to break his power: "…and free those who all their lives were held in slavery by their fear of death" (Hebrews 2:15, NIV).

As long as people are afraid of dying they are in slavery, because the threat of death can compel them to do things they would never otherwise do. The fear of death is the ultimate form of slavery. Jesus came to set us free from that slavery, which is the fear of death. Since we, in our human nature, partake of flesh and blood, He shared our humanity: "For this very reason he had to be made like his brothers in every way…" (Hebrews 2:17, NIV).

So Jesus became like us in every way. Without ceasing to be divine, He became human. He became a member of the human race, the Son of Man. In this way, He was qualified to be what the Bible calls our "kinsman-redeemer." This is a very important concept introduced in the Old Testament but carried on in the New.

WHAT IS A KINSMAN-REDEEMER?

I need to give you a brief explanation of the "kinsman redeemer." We have a problem because in most of the English versions, the Hebrew word is translated differently in different contexts. The Hebrew word is *ga'al*. It is translated variously, as: *avenger* or *revenger of blood, redeemer, next* or *near kinsman*. As "redeemer", this Hebrew word *ga'al* is applied to God Himself almost twenty times in the Old Testament.

Under the Law of Moses and in the culture of Israel in the Old Testament, the kinsman-redeemer had two main responsibilities. If a man had been murdered, the first responsibility of the kinsman redeemer was to follow up the murderer and put him to death. Then if the murdered person was married and died without offspring, the kinsman redeemer was expected to take his widow as wife and raise up descendants for the dead man. This first responsibility is stated in Numbers 35:19: "The avenger of blood [the *ga'al*] himself shall put the murderer to death; when he meets him, he shall put him to death."

The second responsibility of the *ga'al* or the kinsman-redeemer is illustrated in the story of Ruth. Ruth the Moabitess, followed her mother-in-law, Naomi, when she came back to Bethlehem. Naomi told Ruth that she had a near kinsman whose name was Boaz, a wealthy and influential man. Ruth went to glean in the fields of Boaz, and a relationship was established between them that ended in marriage. However, there were certain steps that had to be taken before Boaz could marry Ruth. Here is just a portion of the third chapter of the book of Ruth. (You might want to read the whole story from your own Bible before proceeding further.)

> When Boaz had finished eating and drinking and was in good spirits, he went over to lie down at the far end of the grain pile. Ruth approached quietly, uncovered his feet and lay down. In the middle of the night something startled the man, and he turned and discovered a woman lying at his feet. "Who are you?" he asked. "I am your servant Ruth," she said. "Spread the corner of your garment over me, since you are a kinsman-redeemer [that is, a *ga'al*]."
>
> Ruth 3:7–9, NIV

Ruth was here claiming that Boaz (whose name means "in him is strength") would fulfill his responsibility as her kinsman-redeemer. However, there was one relative who was more closely related than Boaz, whose name is not given. Boaz reminded this relative that if he wanted to redeem the property, he would also have to marry Ruth. Boaz told him:

> "Naomi, who has come back from Moab, is selling the piece of land that belonged to our brother Elimelech. I thought I should bring the matter to your attention and suggest that you buy it in the presence of these seated here and in the presence of the elders of my people. If you will redeem it, do so. But if you will not, tell me, so I will know. For no one has the right to do it except you, and I am next in line." "I will redeem it," he said. Then Boaz said, "On the day you buy the land from Naomi and from Ruth the Moabitess, you acquire the dead man's widow, in order to maintain the name of the dead with his property." At this, the kinsman-redeemer said, "Then I cannot redeem it because I might endanger my own estate. You redeem it yourself. I cannot do it."
>
> Ruth 4:3–6, NIV

You see, the kinsman-redeemer was required not merely to buy back the property of the dead man, but he also had to marry the dead man's widow and thus raise up descendants bearing his name, that it might not be blotted out in Israel.

So those are the two responsibilities of the *ga'al*, the kinsman-redeemer. First, to avenge the murderer who killed his kinsman; secondly, to buy back his kinsman's inheritance and marry his kinsman's widow and raise up descendants who would carry on the family name.

We have seen that Jesus came as our *ga'al*, or our kinsman-redeemer. How did He fulfill His responsibilities in that capacity? First of all, He went against the murderer, Satan, and put an end to his power over us. So He was the avenger of our blood, the avenger against the one who was responsible for our death. Second, He took the church to Himself as His bride, just as Boaz married Ruth, and thus He restored to us our lost inheritance. This part of the picture is illustrated in Romans, where Paul says:

> Therefore, my brethren, you also have become dead to the law through the body of Christ, that you may be married to another – to Him who was raised from the dead, that we should bear fruit to God. For when we were in the flesh, the sinful passions which were aroused by the law were at work in our members to bear fruit to death. But now we have been delivered from the law, having died to what we were held by, so that we should serve in newness of the Spirit and not in the oldness of the letter.
>
> Romans 7:4–6

JESUS AS OUR KINSMAN-REDEEMER

Let us now see how this picture of Jesus as our kinsman-redeemer applies to us in the New Testament. Paul says that in a certain sense, we were married to the law, but through the death of Jesus on the cross, we were set free from that obligation to the law. Therefore, we are now free to be married to another, to Jesus, the one who rose from the dead, our kinsman-redeemer. However, just as in the case of Ruth and Boaz, there was one other who had the legal right to be the redeemer. That was our carnal nature. But our carnal nature, the flesh, was unwilling and unable to help. So, like Ruth, we had to turn to our heavenly Boaz, Christ, who took us to Himself as His bride. He did for us what Boaz did for Ruth. Through our union with Him, our inheritance is restored to us and we bring forth fruit pleasing to God.

In that Old Testament custom or pattern of the kinsman-redeemer, we see illuminated through the Holy Spirit the beautiful picture of Jesus as our kinsman-redeemer, the One who came to avenge our death at the hand of Satan. This He did by taking our death upon Himself, by paying our penalty. In this way, He set us free from the fear of death. And by taking us to Himself as His bride, He restored us to our inheritance.

You remember that Satan was the thief who came to steal. But Jesus said, "I have come that they may have life, and that they may have it more abundantly." So Jesus gave us back our inheritance. He took us to Himself as His bride. We are delivered from the bondage of the law and delivered from the fear of death. We are no longer kept in slavery because of the continual threat of death. The fear of death has been taken from us, and instead we have a new inheritance, an eternal inheritance in Jesus Christ.

In our relationship to Jesus as the bridegroom of our soul, we no longer bring forth the sinful acts produced under the law by our carnal nature. Instead, we bring forth the fruits of righteousness. We become pleasing and acceptable to God. Condemnation is gone. Fear is gone. We can say with the apostle John, "The darkness is passing away, and the true light is already shining" (1 John 2:8). Our kinsman-redeemer has come and taken us to Himself, avenged the murder and restored to us our rightful inheritance in God's family. Meditate on this picture until it becomes real to you. It is so beautiful.

4

THE ATONEMENT

Now we come to the atonement, which is the work that Jesus accomplished through His death on our behalf. Really, in a sense, the entire revelation of Scripture centers in the atonement. Atonement, itself, is a beautiful word, but many people who use it do not actually know what it means. The word "atonement" is made up of three sections: *at – one –* and *ment.* Atonement is "at–one–ment." Atonement restores the sinner to God's favor. It is a reconciliation, the bringing of God and the sinner, who have been alienated, "at one." It is total reconciliation and union.

One of the vivid pictures that has come to me to illustrate the place of the atonement in the total message of the Gospel is that of a wheel. In a wheel, simplistically speaking, there are three sections: the outer circle, the spokes and the hub. In this picture, the outer circle represents God's complete provision for every area of our lives – spiritual, physical, and material, for time and through eternity. The total provision of God through the Gospel is like that full-orbed circle of the wheel. It covers everything. The spokes that support the outer wheel are the ways that God makes provision. For instance, one spoke would be forgiveness, which gives us peace; another spoke healing, which gives us health; another deliverance, which gives us liberty; and another would be sanctification, which gives us holiness. In that way, the spokes support the outer rim, which is God's provision. But the hub, the very center, is the atonement. The spokes rest upon the hub. Without the hub they have nothing to support them. Also, through the hub comes the driving power that turns the wheel.

In God's provision, the atonement is the hub, the center of the wheel. It is that on which everything else depends – that through which the power for the Christian life is supplied.

> But we see Jesus, who was made a little lower than the angels, for the suffering of death crowned with glory and honor, that He, by the grace of God, might taste death for everyone.
>
> Hebrews 2:9

Notice that last phrase: "...that He [Jesus], by the grace of God, might taste death for everyone." He tasted our death; He took our place. That which was due to us came upon Him. This is stated again in Isaiah:

> All of us like sheep have gone astray,
> Each of us has turned to his own way;
> But the Lord has caused the iniquity of us all
> To fall on Him [Jesus].
>
> Isaiah 53:6, NAS

The word that is translated *iniquity* also has the meaning of "rebellion." The rebellion of the whole human race is summed up in that phrase. Each one of us has turned to his own way. We have turned our backs on God, and we have gone our own way. We have done our own thing. We have set our own standards, pleased ourselves, and lived for ourselves. In a word, we have been rebellious. But the Lord made the rebellion of us all to meet together upon Jesus. As Jesus hung there on the cross, all our rebellion was laid upon Him. And then, upon Him as He hung there, came all the evil consequences of rebellion: sickness, rejection, pain, agony, and finally death. But He did not die for Himself; He died our death. He tasted death in our place. He was our Kinsman-redeemer.

ATONEMENT PROPHECIES

In the verses that follow Isaiah 53:6, we have through prophetic inspiration a vivid and detailed description of the suffering of Jesus, written more than seven hundred years before it actually took place.

> He was oppressed and He was afflicted,
> Yet He did not open His mouth;
> Like a lamb that is led to slaughter,
> And like a sheep that is silent before its shearers,
> So He did not open His mouth.
> By oppression and judgment He was taken away;
> And as for His generation, who considered
> That He was cut off out of the land of the living,
> For the transgression of my people to whom the stroke
>   was due?
> His grave was assigned to be with wicked men,
> Yet with a rich man in His death;
> Although He had done no violence,
> Nor was there any deceit in His mouth.
>
> verses 7–9, NAS

Let us look at some of the details that were so accurately fulfilled in the sufferings and the death of Jesus. First of all, "He did not open His mouth." It is emphasized several times in the Gospels that He made no attempt to answer His accusers or justify Himself or plead His own cause. "He did not open His mouth." Then, "By oppression and judgment He was taken away." Unjust accusation and unfair trial led to His death. Then again, "He was cut off out of the land of the living." His accusation and trial ended in His death.

Also the details of His burial are so amazingly accurate. "His grave was assigned to be with wicked men, yet with a rich man in His death." We move from the plural "with wicked men," to the singular "with a rich man." Historically, we find that Jesus was taken down for burial with the two thieves, the two wicked men who were hung on either side of Him, but then He was buried in the tomb of a rich man, Joseph of Arimathea. Such amazing accuracy!

Then it is emphasized again that His sufferings were not for His own sin or guilt. "He had done no violence, nor was there any deceit in His mouth." He was totally innocent, and yet He died the death of a criminal.

The verses that follow show how the purpose of God was fulfilled in the death of Jesus:

> But the Lord was pleased
> To crush Him, putting Him to grief;
> If He would render Himself as a guilt offering,
> He will see His offspring,
> He will prolong His days,
> And the good pleasure of the Lord will prosper in His
>   hand.
> As a result of the anguish of His soul,
> He will see it and be satisfied;

By His knowledge the Righteous One,
My Servant, will justify the many,
As He will bear their iniquities.
Therefore, I will allot Him a portion with the great,
And He will divide the booty with the strong;
Because He poured out Himself to death,
And was numbered with the transgressors;
Yet He Himself bore the sin of many,
And interceded for the transgressors.

verses 10–12, NAS

Again we look at the amazing accuracy of those details. In verse ten, the divine purpose for the death of Jesus is stated, He "render[ed] Himself as a guilt offering." He became the guilt (or sin) offering for the entire human race.

In the words that follow in verse ten, we see that His resurrection is there predicted, "He will see His offspring, He will prolong His days, and the good pleasure of the Lord will prosper in His hand." Already it has been stated that He was to be cut off out of the land of the living, and yet now it is stated that He will see His offspring, and prolong His days. That can only be through resurrection.

Then, in the latter half of verse eleven it says, "By His knowledge the Righteous One, My Servant, will justify the many, as He will bear their iniquities." Because Jesus bore our iniquities and took the penalty of our rebellion; therefore He is now able to offer us His righteousness. He is able to *justify* us.

Finally, in the twelfth verse we read that "He poured out *Himself* to death." But where this translation says "Himself," the Hebrew says "His soul" (see also the NKJ version). Compare that with the statement in Leviticus 17:11: "For the life of the flesh is in the blood, and I have given it to you on the altar to make atonement for your souls; for it is the blood by reason of the life that makes atonement" (NAS).

Now, where this translation says "life," the Hebrew word is "soul": "... the life [soul] of the flesh is in the blood." So, when Jesus poured out His last drop of blood on the cross, He poured out His soul. He yielded up His soul as the atonement, the sin offering. He died our death. He became our sin offering. Then, brought back from the dead, He is able to impart to us His righteousness. "He will see His offspring." We, who through faith in Him, come to God and are born anew, become His offspring. "He will prolong His days" – forever and ever. He is raised again to eternal life. "The good pleasure of the Lord will prosper in His hand." He becomes the instrument to fulfill all God's purposes in the earth.

Especially meditate on the statement that "He poured out Himself [His soul] to death." He poured out His blood. I do not know if you have ever realized that when the blood of Jesus was shed on the cross, the entire life of Almighty God was given forth for the redemption of this world. There is more power in one drop of the blood of Jesus than in all the forces of sin and iniquity in this whole world. When Jesus gave Himself up on the cross, when He poured out His soul with the shedding of His blood, He made available to us the entire riches and resources of the eternal and endless life of God. Then, when He rose from the dead, He came to offer us peace and total pardon. That is how, as our kinsman-redeemer, He defeated our enemy and restored us to our inheritance.

5

The Resurrection

The greatest event of all history up to this time is the resurrection of Jesus Christ. It is the heart of the Christian message. In fact, without the resurrection there is no Christian message. It all revolves around the death and the resurrection of Jesus Christ.

This is not a philosophy or a theory, but a fact of history. Either it is a fact, or it is of no consequence whatsoever. If it is just a theory or a philosophy, it has no power to help humanity. But thank God, it is a fact of history.

> Moreover, brethren, I declare to you the gospel which I preached to you, which also you received and in which you stand, by which also you are saved, if you hold fast that word which I preached to you – unless you believed in vain. For I delivered to you first of all that which I also received: that Christ died for our sins according to the Scriptures, and that He was buried, and that He rose again the third day according to the Scriptures....
>
> 1 Corinthians 15:1–4

HISTORICAL FACTS OF THE GOSPEL

The Gospel of Jesus Christ consists of three simple historical facts. Many people only have a very foggy idea of what the Gospel is. They associate it with something that is primarily emotional or subjective, and much so-called preaching of the Gospel centers on the emotional and the subjective. But this is not accurate. The Gospel is based not on something subjective or emotional, but on simple, vital, historical facts – events that have actually taken place in human history and are attested by many reliable witnesses.

Paul states for us the Gospel that he preached – the Gospel that is essential to believe for salvation. It centers, first of all, in the person of Christ. Second, it centers in three great historical facts that relate to Jesus Christ. Without Jesus, there is no Gospel. The Gospel is not a set of human opinions, and it is not a system of theology or philosophy. It is a set of facts that is rooted in history.

What are the three central facts concerning Jesus Christ which make up the Gospel? First, He *died*. Second, He was *buried*. And third, He *rose again* the third day. You need to imprint them on your mind and on your heart in a way that you will never be able to forget, because Paul, in writing to the Corinthian Christians, says, "These are the facts by which you are saved – unless you believed in vain." Paul is saying that if, at any time, they should get away from these basic facts into some kind of religious theories, fantasies, or subjective experiences, then they would have believed in vain. So, take this opportunity, by the power of the Holy Spirit, to indelibly imprint on your heart and mind these three key central facts that make up the Gospel: Christ died, He was buried, and He rose again the third day.

Paul offers two kinds of confirmation of these historical facts. First, they are attested by the prophetic Scriptures of the Old Testament. Second, they are attested by the testimony of many reliable witnesses.

It is very important that we see that the first confirmation of these facts is not the testimony of human witnesses, although that is very important. But the primary confirmation is the prophetic Scriptures of the Old Testament. The entire New Testament continually emphasizes the fact that the Old Testament prophetic Scriptures had to be fulfilled – that not one of them could fail. Jesus said it, His apostles said it, and this theme is woven throughout the entire New Testament – both in the life of Jesus Himself and in the subsequent activities of His apostles and of the early church. Time and time again, one phrase recurs like a refrain, "that it might be fulfilled" – that which the prophets had spoken.

This means that the primary confirmation of the truth of the resurrection is that it had been predicted clearly in the Old Testament Scriptures. So, in the New Testament, we are confronted not by something new or unpredictable. On the contrary, for those who knew the Scriptures of the Old Testament, the resurrection of Christ was predictable. Not only had it been predicted in the Old Testament, but Jesus Himself clearly predicted His own resurrection because He was familiar with the Scriptures of the Old Testament prophets.

Then the second source of confirmation is the testimony of many reliable witnesses who saw Jesus and fellowshipped with Him after He rose from the dead.

So we have three facts: Christ died. He was buried. He rose again. And we have two sources of confirmation: the prophetic

Scriptures of the Old Testament and the testimony of many reliable witnesses.

Let me point out to you five supporting details related to the resurrection that affirm its validity.

1. It was attested by a much greater number of reliable witnesses than would be required to establish a fact in law.
2. It produced a dramatic and permanent change in those witnesses, for which there is no satisfactory alternative explanation.
3. Adhering to their testimony cost many of these witnesses their lives. They had nothing material to gain from it.
4. It has produced a radical and permanent change in the course of history. History will never be the same, and there is no satisfactory alternative explanation for that change.
5. The resurrected Christ has continued to reveal Himself personally as alive to countless millions in the ensuing centuries, and I am one of them.

In 1941, while I was serving as a soldier in the British Army, one night in the barrack room, I had a direct, personal revelation of Jesus. I was not unduly religious. I was not a person who was seeking something special or fanciful or out of order. There was nothing unusual in my psychology at that moment. But Jesus revealed Himself to me so genuinely and so personally that, from that day to this, I have never been able to doubt that He is alive. And, if He is alive, that is the most important fact of history.

How Christianity is Different

In connection with what Paul says about the three facts of the Gospel, let me point out to you three ways in which Christianity, based on these facts, differs from almost every other major religion. The first way is that Christianity is totally centered in a person. That person is Jesus of Nazareth. It is not merely that He was the one who delivered the truths of the Gospel, but it is in His life and death and resurrection that the entire Gospel is centered. You cannot take away Jesus and have the Gospel. You cannot take away Jesus and have the New Testament. Now, that is not true of other religions. You could, for instance, take away Mohammed and replace him with someone else with another name and from another age. This other person could have come out with the same theories, because the Mohammedan religion is based on theories, not historical facts. There are historical facts connected with it, but they are not essential to its truth. In the case of Christianity, however, these historical facts about Jesus are central to its truth. If they had not happened, the Gospel could never have been presented to the human race.

A second distinctive fact about Christianity is that it is rooted in history. As already emphasized, it is not something subjective or theoretical. It is not floating in some misty realm of subjective truth or theory or theology. It is centered directly in human history. If the events on which it is based are true, then Christianity is true. If they are not true, then Christianity is not true. There is nothing in between. It is a complete commitment to a certain set of historical facts.

Third, Christianity claims that it will be verified in the personal experience of those who believe – and base their lives around – these three vital facts: Christ's death, His burial, and His resurrection. Believing in Jesus and in these facts about Jesus will produce a tremendous, supernatural transformation in the lives of everyone who believes.

So again, Christianity is rooted in human experience. It is rooted in the personal history of everyone who believes it and receives it. That takes it out of the realm of theory. This is important to note because so many people today view Christianity as just one religion among many – one set of theories or one set of moral principles. That is incorrect. Christianity is different from the religions that are theories or moral principles because it is based directly in human history and in human experience. It stands or falls with the truth of history and of human experience.

WHY MEN REJECT CHRISTIANITY

I have established that the resurrection of Jesus Christ is a historical fact and yet, of course, there are many who reject it. Why do they reject it? Why will they not receive the evidence? I suggest to you that there are two main reasons. The first is psychological, the second is spiritual. Psychologically, people do not wish to acknowledge the possibility of God's direct, supernatural intervention in human affairs. They resent the thought that somehow God can change what they regard as a fixed course of events. And yet, there are no logical or scientific reasons for this attitude. I dare to speak with some authority because at one time I myself was a professor of philosophy, and one of the subjects that I studied in some detail was the logic of science. I would venture to say that science can offer no logical reason why the resurrection of Jesus Christ should not have taken place. It is not scientific to assert that it did not happen. In fact, it is unscientific to reject the valid evidence that it did happen.

The second reason why people find it hard to believe in the resurrection of Jesus is spiritual. This is stated clearly by Paul in 2 Corinthians 4:4: "The god of this age has blinded the minds of unbelievers, so that they cannot see the light of the gospel of the glory of Christ, who is the image of God" (NIV).

In Scripture, the "god of this age" is one of the many titles of Satan. As we have said, Satan is the murderer, the thief, the life-taker, while Jesus is the life-giver. On the cross, Jesus met and conquered Satan. He defeated him finally and forever. Since that time, Satan has no answer to the cross. It spells his defeat. It ends his power to dominate humanity and inflict upon them his cruel will and the endless agonies for which he is responsible – emotional, physical, and spiritual. Therefore, Satan now has one supreme objective: to keep men and women from understanding the truth of what happened when Jesus died and rose from the dead.

Paul says that, as the god of this age, he has blinded the minds of unbelievers. That is why they cannot see the clear, plain truth, the message of salvation and deliverance that is given to us through Jesus Christ.

LOGICAL AND NECESSARY

From God's viewpoint the resurrection of Jesus was both logical and necessary. It was God's vindication of the obedience and righteousness of His Son, Jesus. Paul states this in the opening verses of Romans:

> Paul, a servant of Christ Jesus, called to be an apostle and set apart for the gospel of God – the gospel he promised beforehand through his prophets in the Holy Scriptures regarding his Son, who as to his human nature was a descendant of David, and who through the Spirit of holiness was declared with power to be the Son of God by his resurrection from the dead: Jesus Christ our Lord.
>
> Romans 1:1–4, NIV

In the flesh Jesus was a descendant of David, but in His eternal nature He was the Son of God and our Lord. God declared that Jesus was His Son by raising Him from the dead. The resurrection is God's great vindication of His Son. It is the public demonstration to the universe that Jesus – though He died a criminal's death and was rejected by man – was indeed, and is, the Son of God and our Lord. This is summed up in a paragraph from my book *Foundational Truths For Christian Living* in the section titled "Resurrection of the Dead":

> Previously, Christ had been brought before two human courts – first, the religious court of the Jewish council, and then the secular court of the Roman governor, Pontius Pilate. Both these courts had rejected Jesus' claim to be the Son of God and had condemned Him to death. Furthermore, both these courts had united in seeking to prevent any breaking open of the grave of Jesus. To this end, the Jewish council had provided their special seal, and the Roman governor had provided an armed guard of soldiers.
>
> However, on the third day God intervened. The seal was broken, the armed guard was paralyzed, and Jesus came forth from the tomb. By this act God reversed the decisions of the Jewish council and the Roman governor, and He publicly vindicated the claim of Christ to be the sinless Son of God.
>
> pages 464–465

The justice of God was vindicated by the resurrection of Jesus. Jesus had been set aside by humanity as a criminal, but God, by the resurrection, endorsed His claim to be the Son of God.

What should our response be? Here is a beautiful passage describing the response of the women who were the first witnesses of the resurrection:

So they went out quickly from the tomb with fear and great joy, and ran to bring His disciples word. And as they went to tell His disciples, behold, Jesus met them, saying, "Rejoice!" So they came and held Him by the feet and worshiped Him.

Matthew 28:8–9

What else can we do when we realize who He is and what He did? There is no other reasonable response but to do as those women did: fall at His feet and worship Him.

6

ACCORDING TO THE SCRIPTURES

The Scriptures of the Old Testament show us how the resurrection was clearly predicted. As well as increasing our understanding of the resurrection, they also provide an outstanding example of the amazing accuracy of biblical prophecy.

We have already looked at what Paul states is the essence of the gospel:

> For I delivered to you first of all that which I also received: that Christ died for our sins according to the Scriptures, and that He was buried, and that He rose again on the third day according to the Scriptures.
>
> 1 Corinthians 15:3–4

From verse four, we have to understand that "the Scriptures" means what we would call the Old Testament. In the time that Paul was writing, the New Testament was not yet a complete or established book of Scripture. Paul says the Gospel consists of three historical facts: Christ died for our sins, He was buried, and He rose again on the third day. He also says that the highest single authority for each of these statements is that they were the fulfillment of Old Testament prophecies – that is, "according to the Scriptures." He places the authority of the Scriptures before that of the eyewitnesses of the resurrection whom he then proceeds to quote. The primary confirmation of Christ's resurrection is to be found in the prophetic Scriptures of the Old Testament. It is natural to ask ourselves, what Scriptures did Paul have in mind? What passages of the Old Testament predicted the resurrection of Jesus Christ?

FACTS ABOUT OLD TESTAMENT PROPHECY

Before we answer this question, however, we need to understand a principle of interpretation of Old Testament prophecy when it relates to Christ. The apostle Peter states this principle:

> Of this salvation the prophets have inquired and searched carefully, who prophesied of the grace that would come to you, searching what, or what manner of time, the Spirit of Christ who was in them [notice that phrase, the Spirit of Christ was in the Old Testament prophets] was indicating when He testified beforehand the sufferings of Christ and the glories that would follow. To them it was revealed that, not to themselves, but to us they were ministering the things which now have been reported to you through those who have preached the gospel to you by the Holy Spirit sent from heaven – things which angels desire to look into.
>
> 1 Peter 1:10–12

We need to bear in mind three essential facts about Old Testament prophecy:

1. The Spirit of Christ, the Messiah, in the first person, spoke through the Old Testament prophets.
2. The Spirit of Christ in them predicted two things concerning Christ the Messiah: first, His sufferings and, second, the glories that would follow out of His sufferings.
3. Their message was not for their own generation, but for believers in the New Testament.

PROPHECIES FULFILLED

Now we will look at two specific examples of this from the writings of the prophet David in the book of Psalms. Bear in mind that the New Testament calls David a prophet. Much of what is written by David and by others in the Psalms is prophecy. Our first example is taken from Psalm 22:16–18:

> For dogs have surrounded Me;
> The congregation of the wicked has enclosed Me.
> They pierced My hands and My feet;
> I can count all My bones.
> They look and stare at Me.
> They divide My garments among them,
> And for My clothing they cast lots.
>
> Psalm 22:16–18

David lists a series of experiences that he describes in the first person, yet which never happened to him. "They pierced My hands and My feet." That did not happen to David. "They divide My garments among them." That did not happen to David. "For my clothing they cast lots." That did not happen to David, and yet David spoke in the first person. What is the explanation? It is given by the apostle Peter in 1 Peter 1:10–12. It was the Spirit of

Christ (the Messiah) speaking through the prophets (of whom David was one) and describing experiences that never happened to the prophets who spoke them, but that were to be fulfilled in the experience of Jesus.

> Reproach has broken my heart,
> And I am full of heaviness;
> I looked for someone to take pity, but there was
>   none;
> And for comforters, but I found none.
> They also gave me gall for my food,
> And for my thirst they gave me vinegar to drink.
>
> Psalm 69:20–21

Again, David speaks here in the first person and describes things that never happened in his experience, "For my thirst they gave me vinegar to drink." There is no record that ever happened to David, yet the experience he describes did happen to Jesus, and it is carefully recorded in the New Testament. Many of these events out of the writings of David in the Psalms were fulfilled – not in his experience, but in the experience of Jesus in the New Testament.

> They gave Him [Jesus] sour wine [vinegar] mingled with gall to drink. But when He had tasted it, He would not drink. Then they crucified Him, and divided His garments, casting lots, that it might be fulfilled which was spoken by the prophet.
>
> Matthew 27:34–35

Notice that the details David wrote about himself in the first person that were not fulfilled in his experience *were* fulfilled in the crucifixion of Christ. Also the writer of this portion of the

New Testament says they happened that it might be fulfilled which was spoken by the prophet. In other words, this was the outworking of the prophecies of the Old Testament.

Another example of the same principle is found in the prophecies of Isaiah. In other words, the Spirit of Christ, the Messiah, speaking through Isaiah in the first person, of things which never happened to Isaiah, but which were fulfilled in Jesus.

> The Lord God has opened My ear;
> And I was not rebellious,
> Nor did I turn away.
> I gave My back to those who struck Me,
> And My cheeks to those who plucked out the
>   beard;
> I did not hide My face from shame and spitting.
>
> Isaiah 50:5–6

There is no record or suggestion that any of this ever happened in the experience of Isaiah, and yet he speaks in the first person as though it had. What is the explanation? It was the Spirit of Christ, the Messiah, in Isaiah, speaking of what was to be fulfilled in the experience of Jesus. Again, the New Testament very carefully records the fulfillment of these events.

First of all, speaking about Jesus after He had been arrested, Matthew wrote, "Then they spat in His face and beat Him; and others struck Him with the palms of their hands" (Matthew 26:67). Then we read in Isaiah 50:6, "I gave my cheeks to those who plucked out the beard; I did not hide My face from shame and spitting," which was fulfilled exactly in the experience of Jesus, not of Isaiah (see Mark 14:65, 15:20). We read again concerning Jesus, "Then [Pontius Pilate] released Barabbas to them; and when he had scourged Jesus, he delivered Him to be crucified" (Matthew 27:26). Notice Jesus was scourged before He was crucified. It had to be so because of what Isaiah said in chapter 50, "I gave My back to those who struck Me." In the scourging of Jesus, those words were fulfilled. They were not fulfilled in Isaiah, but they were fulfilled in Jesus.

RESURRECTION PREDICTED

I want to develop this theme further and to share with you two specific predictions of Christ's resurrection from the psalms of David. We are going to apply this principle of Old Testament prophecy to the writings of David in the book of Psalms, and particularly to writings that predicted the resurrection of Jesus.

> I have set the Lord always before me;
> Because He is at my right hand I shall not be
> moved.
> Therefore my heart is glad, and my glory rejoices;
> My flesh also will rest in hope.
> For You will not leave my soul in Sheol,
> Nor will You allow Your Holy One to see
> corruption.
> You will show me the path of life;
> In Your presence is fullness of joy;
> At Your right hand are pleasures forevermore.
>
> Psalm 16:8–11

Notice that all the way through, David is speaking in the first person, and yet there are many things he says that were not fulfilled in his experience. He says, first of all, "My flesh also will rest in hope." Here he speaks about a body that is to be buried, but buried in hope of resurrection. Then he says, "You will not leave my soul in Sheol." He is speaking of someone whose soul descended into Sheol – that is, the place of the departed spirits – but did not remain there. "Nor will You allow Your Holy One to see corruption." Here he is speaking about someone whose body was buried but never underwent the experience of corruption, and this person is here called God's "Holy One." In the following verse he says, "You will show me the path of life." So here is someone who has been dead and buried and yet comes back into the path of life. Then he says, "In Your [God's] presence is fullness of joy; at Your right hand are pleasures forevermore." This person who has died and been buried and come back to life is brought into the immediate presence of God and takes His place at God's right hand.

None of those things happened to David, but all of them happened to Jesus.

In Acts chapter two, the apostle Peter, speaking to a large crowd of Jewish people on the Day of Pentecost, specifically applies this prophecy of David to Jesus:

God raised [Jesus] up, having loosed the pains of death, because it was not possible that He should be held by it. For David says concerning Him:
  "I foresaw the Lord always before my face,
   For He is at my right hand, that I may not be shaken.
   Therefore my heart rejoiced, and my tongue was glad;
   Moreover my flesh will also rest in hope,
   For You will not leave my soul in Hades [the Greek
     name for Sheol],
   Nor will you allow Your Holy One to see corruption.
   You have made known to me the ways of life;
   You will make me full of joy in Your presence."

Acts 2:24–28

Then in the following verses, Peter goes on to interpret these words and show how they applied exactly to Jesus but did not apply to David.

> Men and brethren, let me speak freely to you of the patriarch David, that he is both dead and buried, and his tomb is with us to this day. [So here is the historical evidence that these words concerning resurrection were not fulfilled in the experience of David. He says, "I can take you to the tomb and show you where he was buried and from which he was not resurrected."] Therefore, being a prophet, and knowing that God had sworn with an oath to him that of the fruit of his body, according to the flesh, He would raise up the Christ [the Messiah] to sit on his throne, he, foreseeing this, spoke concerning the resurrection of the Christ [the Messiah], that His soul was not left in Hades, nor did His flesh see corruption. "This Jesus God has raised up, of which we all are witnesses."
>
> Acts 2:29–33

Peter is saying is that all this did not happen to David, but it happened exactly to Jesus. Prophetically, what David was saying in the Psalm was fulfilled in the resurrection of Christ. It was Christ's soul that descended into Hades but was not left there, and it was Christ's flesh in the tomb that never saw corruption. Peter sums it up with these powerful words, "This Jesus God has raised up, of which we all are witnesses."

The predication of Jesus' resurrection as we have seen it in Psalm 16 can be summed up as follows:

- It was quoted in the New Testament by Peter and Paul, and by each of them applied to Jesus.

- It did not apply to David.
- It indicated that the soul of Jesus would descend into Sheol (or Hades), but not remain there.
- The body of Jesus would lie in the tomb but would not undergo decay.
- Through resurrection, Jesus would be restored to the presence of God the Father.

Let's explore one other passage in the book of Psalms where again David is speaking in the first person. He is speaking of that which did not happen to him, but that which was exactly fulfilled in the experience of the Messiah who was, of course, descended from David's line. The psalmist is speaking to God and he says:

> You, who have shown me great and severe troubles,
> Shall revive me again,
> And bring me up again from the depths of the earth.
> You shall increase my greatness,
> And comfort me on every side.

Psalm 71:20–21

It is truly amazing how exactly that predicts, step by step and phase by phase, the experience of Jesus. Let us look first at the order of events recorded in this Psalm. First of all, "You have shown me great and severe troubles." Certainly that was fulfilled in Jesus – in His trial, rejection, scourging, and ultimately crucifixion and death. But then the psalmist goes on, "You... shall revive me again and bring me up again from the depths of the earth." This describes two events: the soul of Jesus being recalled from Hades or Sheol, and His body being brought back out of the tomb. That is one of clearest statements of physical resurrection that is to be found anywhere in the Old Testament. It says, "You will bring me up again from the depths of the earth." First, however, God had to revive Him – bring Him back to life. Then He brought Him up again out of the tomb. That is the same order that is emphasized also in the New Testament.

Then, after resurrection, the psalmist goes on to say, "You shall increase my greatness, and comfort me on every side." Again, the New Testament exactly records how that was fulfilled in the experience of Jesus. God not merely resurrected Him, but He raised Him up to heaven and gave Him a seat at His right hand on the throne, by His side. Surely that was increasing His greatness. The New Testament says that He has been exalted far above every principality and power and might and dominion, and every name that is named, and that angels and principalities and powers have been made subject to Him (see Ephesians 1:20–23, Romans 8:38). Surely His greatness was increased, but the psalmist also says, "You shall . . . comfort me on every side." Not merely did Jesus receive the position of supreme authority and honor in the universe, but also He was comforted by His restoration to the bosom of the Father from whom He had been separated briefly for the sufferings of death.

We can summarize that in two statements: Jesus endured great and sore troubles, but He was restored to life again. He was brought up from the depths of the earth, and He was restored to His place of honor at God's right hand.

Predicted by Hosea

Our next prediction of Christ's resurrection is found in the prophet Hosea. This passage in Hosea has a unique feature: it is given in the first person *plural*, not singular. Hosea uses the word *we*, not *I*.

Before we examine those verses, however, I want to suggest that Paul referred to the prophecy of Hosea in 1 Corinthians 15:3–4:

> For I delivered to you first of all that which I also received: that Christ died for our sins according to the Scriptures, and that He was buried, and that He rose again the third day according to the Scriptures...

Notice the closing phrase there, "He rose again *the third day* according to the Scriptures." Paul emphasizes first, that He rose on the third day and, second, His rising on the third day was a fulfillment of the Old Testament Scriptures. This Scripture attaches considerable importance to the fact that it was predicted that Jesus would be resurrected on the third day.

This raises a very significant question: Which Old Testament Scripture was fulfilled by Jesus' rising on the third day? One Scripture that emphasizes the third day is found in Hosea 6:1–2:

> Come, and let us return to the Lord;
> For He has torn, but He will heal us;
> He has stricken, but He will bind us up. [Ultimately,
>   this is a promise of healing and restoration.]
> After two days He will revive us;
> On the third day He will raise us up,
> That we may live in His sight.

Notice the clear emphasis: "After two days He will revive us [bring us back to life]; on the third day He will raise us up." That was exactly fulfilled in Jesus after two days. God revived Him on the third day; He raised Him up from the tomb. But, the significant feature there is that Hosea speaks about *us*, not just about *me*. In other words, though it refers to Jesus, it is not limited to Jesus.

There is an important principle at work here: Old Testament prophecy not merely predicts facts, but it also reveals the spiritual significance of the facts that it states. This is particularly true in this prophecy of Hosea. Hosea is predicting, first of all, that the resurrection of Jesus will take place on the third day, but second, He goes beyond that and implies that Jesus' resurrection, in some sense, will also be our resurrection – that we, believers, are identified with Jesus in resurrection.

IDENTIFIED WITH CHRIST

Our identification with Christ is clearly brought out in the New Testament. This is a two-way identification. First, Jesus identified Himself with us by becoming human. He became the sinner's substitute, and He took the sinner's place. Our salvation only comes, however, when we, in turn, identify ourselves with Him – first in death, then in resurrection. In Ephesians 2:4–6 Paul depicts the climax of this identification:

> But God, who is rich in mercy, because of His great love with which He loved us, even when we were dead in trespasses, *made us alive together* with Christ (by grace you have been saved), and *raised us up together*, and *made us sit together* in heavenly places in Christ Jesus...
>
> (*emphasis added*)

Notice the word *together*, which occurs three times in succession. These are three experiences that we share with Jesus. First, we are made alive; second, we are raised up (or resurrected); and third, we are made to sit together in heavenly places, enthroned with Him.

Jesus identified Himself with us in our sin and paid the penalty for our sin by His death. After that, however, in all His subsequent experiences – burial, resurrection, and ascension – we are, by faith, identified with Jesus. This is the message of Hosea.

Furthermore, the New Testament makes it clear and very specific that the outward act of our identification with Jesus is baptism. This is stated in Colossians 2:12: "You were buried with Him in baptism, in which you also were raised with Him through faith in the working of God, who raised Him from the dead."

So, first and foremost, we are identified with Jesus in His burial by baptism, but, being identified with Him in His burial, we are also identified with Him in His resurrection: "Therefore we were buried with Him through baptism into death, that just as Christ was raised from the dead by the glory of the Father, even so we also should walk in newness of life" (Romans 6:4).

The principle is that when we believe and are baptized, then we are identified with Jesus in burial. Being identified with Him in burial, we then go through – with Him – every subsequent experience. We are made alive. We are resurrected. And we are enthroned. Notice how much significance this adds to the ordinance of baptism.

WHAT FOLLOWS RESURRECTION

Now I want to return to the prophecy of Hosea. Let's explore what follows the predictive passage that we have already looked at:

> Come, and let us return to the Lord;
> For He has torn, but He will heal us;
> He has stricken, but He will bind us up.
> After two days He will revive us;
> On the third day He will raise us up,
> That we may live in His sight.

> Hosea 6:1–2

I pointed out that this was fulfilled in the experience of Jesus, but Hosea takes this a step further. Hosea foresees – by the Holy Spirit – that we who believe will be identified with Jesus in the experience of resurrection on the third day. He then continues:

> Let us know,
> Let us pursue the knowledge of the Lord.
> His going forth is established as the morning;
> He will come to us like the rain,
> Like the latter and former rain to the earth.

verse 3

Hosea gives here a further revelation of what is to follow the resurrection of Jesus, but this revelation is only for those who follow on, who pursue the knowledge of God. It is not for those who just skim through Scriptures, but it is for those who read Scripture with an open heart and mind, seeking the truth that God desires to reveal. It is significant that the earthly life of Jesus was witnessed by all alike – believers and unbelievers, friends and enemies. However, from the moment of His resurrection onwards, the revelation of His resurrection and all that followed was granted only to those who met the scriptural requirements: they "knew and pursued the knowledge of the Lord." For those who follow on, who pursue the knowledge of God, two further statements are made.

First, "His going forth is established as the morning." This is referring to His going forth from the tomb. It is compared to the sunrise. Then after resurrection it says, "He will come to us like the rain, like the latter and former rain to the earth." All through the Scriptures, particularly in the book of the prophet Joel, which follows Hosea, the coming of the rain to the earth is a picture of the coming down of the Holy Spirit upon the people of God. Following resurrection, there is to be a coming down of the Holy Spirit like the rain. That was fulfilled fifty days after resurrection, on the Day of Pentecost. So you can see how wonderfully accurate and how revelatory this prediction is.

- It predicts that Jesus will be raised up the third day.
- It predicts our identification with Jesus in His resurrection.
- It predicts that His resurrection will be like a dawn, and, of course, it did happen just about the time of dawn. It was a dawn after the long darkness of sin and death.
- It predicts that God will come back to His people in the Holy Spirit, like the rain. This was fulfilled on the Day of Pentecost.

In our next chapter we will look at some of those who were witnesses of the resurrection.

7

WITNESSES OF THE RESURRECTION

We have examined the primary confirmation of Christ's resurrection: the prophetic Scriptures of the Old Testament. We have also looked in some detail at a number of passages that predicted Christ's resurrection in accurate detail.

Now we turn to the second main confirmation of Christ's resurrection: the witnesses who saw Him alive after His resurrection. Let's look again at 1 Corinthians:

> For I delivered to you first of all that which I also received: that Christ died for our sins according to the Scriptures, and that He was buried, and that He rose again the third day according to the Scriptures, and that He was seen by Cephas [that is, Peter], then by the twelve. After that He was seen by over five hundred brethren at once, of whom the greater part remain to the present, but some have fallen asleep. After that He was seen by James, then by all the apostles. Then last of all He was seen by me also, as one born out of due time.
>
> 1 Corinthians 15:3–8

THE WITNESSES

Paul states there the three central facts of the Gospel: Christ died, He was buried, and He rose again. The first confirmation of the resurrection is that it was a fulfillment of the prophetic Scriptures of the Old Testament. Then Paul gave us the second source of confirmation, that is, the witnesses who saw Jesus alive after His resurrection.

According to Jewish law, which was in force in the time of Jesus and the apostles, to establish the truth of a statement in a court of law it was necessary to produce two, or preferably three, reliable male witnesses. This principle is stated many times in the Old Testament, confirmed also in the New. But in this passage in 1 Corinthians, Paul actually gives more than five hundred such witnesses.

Let us look at the list of witnesses that he gives. First of all, in verse five, he says that Cephas (the apostle Peter) saw Him. This is referred to in Luke's Gospel, where it speaks about the two who were on the road to Emmaus, when Jesus, in a form they did not at first recognize, joined Himself with them. However, when He went in with them and they broke bread together, He was revealed to them and at that moment He disappeared.

> So they rose up that very hour and returned to Jerusalem, and found the eleven and those who were with them gathered together, saying, "The Lord is risen indeed, and has appeared to Simon!"
>
> Luke 24:33–34

So the eleven and those who were gathered with them knew at that time what Paul states in 1 Corinthians 15 – that one of the first appearances of the Lord after His resurrection was to Simon Peter (or Cephas).

Then Paul says, He was also seen by "the twelve"; that is, the apostles. Various such appearances are mentioned in the New Testament. Luke, the writer of Acts, says this concerning the earthly life and ministry of Jesus:

> The former account [the Gospel of Luke] I made, O Theophilus, of all that Jesus began both to do and teach, until the day in which He was taken up [to heaven], after He through the Holy Spirit had given commandments to the apostles whom He had chosen, to whom He also presented Himself alive after His suffering by many infallible proofs, being seen by them during forty days and speaking of the things pertaining to the kingdom of God.
>
> Acts 1:1–3

So Luke says that Jesus presented Himself alive to His apostles after His resurrection and demonstrated that He was alive by many infallible proofs, as indicated in the Gospel of John:

> Then, the same day at evening, being the first day of the week, when the doors were shut where the disciples were assembled, for fear of the Jews, Jesus came and stood in the midst, and said to them, "Peace be with you." When He had said this, He showed them His hands and His side. Then the disciples were glad when they saw the Lord. Then Jesus said to them again, "Peace to you! As the Father has sent Me, I also send you."
>
> John 20:19–21

Jesus, in His resurrection body, had the power to pass through locked doors and present Himself inside the room. First, He bestowed His peace upon His disciples, and then it says specifically, "He showed them His hands and His side," with the marks of crucifixion still visible. He did that to prove that the body that He had was the same body that had been crucified and then resurrected.

Then, in the list of witnesses given in 1 Corinthians 15, Paul states there was a group of more than five hundred believers at one time. This is not described anywhere else in the New Testament. All we know about it is contained in 1 Corinthians 15:6. It seems probable to me that it happened in Galilee because the Scripture says that Jesus made an appointment with His disciples to meet them in Galilee after the resurrection. Then in verse seven of that chapter, Paul says that Jesus appeared to James – that is, James, the brother of the Lord.

Now this is not described elsewhere in the New Testament, but we note the subsequent testimony of James himself in James 1:1, where he introduces himself as, "James a bondservant of God and of the Lord Jesus Christ." During the earthly life of Jesus, James apparently was not a disciple, but in this passage he speaks of himself as a bondservant of the Lord Jesus Christ. So it is clear that Jesus' resurrection appearance had a profound and permanent impact on James.

Then, in verse eight of 1 Corinthians 15, Paul includes himself as the last witness of the resurrection. It is a reference to his experience on the road to Damascus. This is described in Acts 26:8–15, where Paul is speaking to King Agrippa before whom he was on trial:

"Why should it be thought incredible by you that God raises the dead? Indeed, I myself thought I must do many things contrary to the name of Jesus of Nazareth. This I also did in Jerusalem, and many of the saints I shut up in prison, having received authority from the chief priests; and when they were put to death, I cast my vote against them. And I punished them often in every synagogue and compelled them to blaspheme; and being exceedingly enraged against them, I persecuted them even to foreign cities. While thus occupied, as I journeyed to Damascus with authority and commission from the chief priests, at midday, O king, along the road I saw a light from heaven, brighter than the sun, shining around me and those who journeyed with me. And when we had all fallen to the ground, I heard a voice speaking to me and saying in the Hebrew language, 'Saul, Saul, why are you persecuting Me? It is hard for you to kick against the goads.' So I said, 'Who are You, Lord?' And He said, 'I am Jesus, whom you are persecuting.'"

This final revelation of the resurrected Christ was given to His persecutor and enemy, Saul of Tarsus, who became the apostle Paul.

This concludes Paul's list of the various witnesses who saw Jesus alive after His resurrection from the dead. There are actually more than five hundred such witnesses.

COMMON FEATURES OF THE WITNESSES

I want to point out to you certain significant features that are common to these witnesses. First of all, they were men who never failed to record their own weaknesses and failings. One of the amazing things about the Bible, both Old Testament and New, is that the writers honestly recorded their own weaknesses and failings. They were not grandiose or boasters. They were not trying to present a special picture of themselves as a kind of infallible race of superior beings.

Second, all these witnesses were changed from unbelief to

belief. At one time they had not believed in the resurrection, then subsequently they believed. In Paul's case, it was not merely a change from unbelief but from active opposition.

Third, the change was permanent and completely revolutionized their entire lives. They were never the same again after the revelation of the resurrected Christ.

Fourth, no persecution or threat of death could ever cause them to go back on their testimony. They were actually threatened and sometimes punished with death if they would maintain this testimony to the resurrection of Jesus. But no pressure, no persecution could ever cause them to go back on this testimony. They always said, "We have to speak of what we have seen and what we know."

So I ask you, as I have also asked myself: What other explanation could there be of these facts except that their testimony was true? I do not believe there is any other reasonable explanation available except that they were actually testifying to the truth.

I would like to close this chapter with the words of a well-known professor of history from Cambridge University, my alma mater. Professor Marcus Dodds said this: "The resurrection of Jesus is one of the best attested facts of human history."

8

What the Resurrection Means for Us

In chapter three I explained how Jesus, as our kinsman-redeemer, took upon Himself the sentence of death that was due to each of us and yielded up His soul as the sin offering on our behalf, thereby expiating our guilt. Then on the third day, God the Father set aside the unjust decisions of the two human courts (Jewish and Roman) that had condemned Jesus to death, and vindicated the righteousness of his Son by raising Him from the dead. Let's explore just what Christ's resurrection means for each of us.

The Sure Seal

The first thing that we need to see is that the resurrection of Jesus, who was our representative, is the sure seal upon God's offer of forgiveness and salvation through Jesus.

In Romans 4:18–22, Paul explains how Abraham's faith in God's promise was "credited to him as righteousness." Then he continues with an application to us also as believers today:

The words "it was credited to him" were written not for him alone, but also for us, to whom God will credit righteousness – for us who believe in him who raised Jesus our Lord from the dead. He was delivered over to death for our sins and was raised to life for our justification.

Romans 4:23–25, NIV

The word *justification* is a technical theological word. We might render it "acquittal" or "that we might be rendered righteous." Perhaps the best explanation of what it means to be justified is this: Justified means "just-as-if-I'd never sinned," because Christ's sinless righteousness is imputed or credited to us through our faith.

In Romans 4:25 Paul tells us that Christ "was delivered up because of our offenses, and was raised because of our justification." This is evidence that the sinner's justification is dependent upon Christ being raised again from the dead. Had Christ remained upon the cross or in the tomb, God's promise to the sinner of salvation and eternal life could never have been fulfilled. It is only the risen Christ, received and confessed by faith, who brings to the sinner pardon, peace, eternal life and victory over sin: "If you confess with your mouth the Lord Jesus [or Jesus as Lord] and believe in your heart that God has raised Him from the dead, you will be saved" (Romans 10:9).

Here salvation is stated to be dependent upon two things: first, openly confessing Jesus as Lord; second, believing in the heart that God raised Jesus from the dead. Thus, saving faith includes faith in the resurrection. There can be no salvation for those who do not believe in the resurrection of Christ. Logic and intellectual honesty permit no other conclusion. If Christ is not risen from the dead, then He has no power to pardon or to save the sinner. But if He is risen, as the Scripture states, then this is logical proof of His power to pardon and to save. This consequence of Christ's resurrection is clearly set forth in Hebrews 7:25: "Therefore He is also able to save to the uttermost those who come to God through Him, since He always lives to make intercession for them."

The absolute, logical necessity of Christ's resurrection as a basis of God's offer of salvation is stated again by Paul in 1 Corinthians 15:14, 17: "And if Christ is not risen, then our preaching is empty [or vain] and your faith is also empty [or vain].... And if Christ is not risen, your faith is futile; and you are still in your sins."

Some Christians have the attitude that all we receive through salvation is here and now. Specifically, we are going to get healing, prosperity, and all sorts of blessings. But Paul says in 1 Corinthians 15:19 that if our expectations are limited only to this life then "we are of all men the most to be pitied." I feel so sorry for Christians whose hope and expectation is only for this life. They are of all people the most to be pitied. If there is no resurrection, then we are miserable. We have no hope. The grave is our goal, and the grave is our end. But thank God there is a resurrection! Paul explains in Romans 10:9–10 that if you want to be saved, you have to believe in the resurrection:

> That if you confess with your mouth the Lord Jesus and believe in your heart that God has raised Him from the dead, you will be saved. For with the heart one believes unto righteousness, and with the mouth confession is made unto salvation.

If you do not believe that God raised Jesus from the dead, you are a lost soul. You are not saved, and you cannot be saved. No matter how religious you may be, no matter how often you may go to church, if you do not believe personally in the resurrection, you are a lost soul headed for a lost eternity.

Then Paul goes on to argue the case for the resurrection in 1 Corinthians 15:29. He refers to a practice where one believer is baptized by proxy on behalf of another believer: "Otherwise, what will they do who are baptized for the dead, if the dead do not rise at all? Why then are they baptized for the dead?"

I offer no absolutely guaranteed explanation of this passage, but in my understanding it depicts a situation in which a person is saved through faith in Jesus but cannot be baptized. For instance, a criminal awaiting execution is led to the Lord in the execution area, but he cannot be baptized, so another believer can, by proxy, be baptized for him. That is merely "a Prince theory" – you don't have to believe it. But Paul's point is that if there is no resurrection, why should we bother about this man that is being executed?

The condition of contemporary Christendom abundantly confirms these plain statements of Scripture. Those theologians who reject the personal, physical resurrection of Christ may moralize and theorize as much as they please, but one thing they never come to know in personal experience is the peace and the joy of having their sins forgiven.

As I have said previously, Christ's resurrection is the sure seal upon God's offer of forgiveness and salvation to each one of us.

Our Guarantee

The second thing we need to see is that Christ's resurrection is the guarantee of our resurrection: "And He [Jesus] is the head of the body, the church, who is the beginning, the firstborn

from the dead, that in all things He may have the preeminence"
(Colossians 1:18).

Jesus was the beginning of the first creation of God, and
through His resurrection He is also the beginning of the new creation of God, which is made available to us through faith. Here,
in this passage in Colossians, Jesus is said to be the beginning and
the firstborn from the dead. In other words, resurrection is here
compared to a rebirth out of death. This agrees with what we find
in Psalm 2, which is a prophetic preview of the resurrection of the
Lord Jesus. In the verse below, the resurrected Christ is speaking
of the decree that God the Father has made concerning Him.

> I will declare the decree:
> The Lord has said to Me,
> "You are My Son,
> Today I have begotten You."
>
> Psalm 2:7

The day on which the Father begot the Son was the Resurrection Day. Jesus was the first begotten from the dead. His
resurrection was a birth out of death to a new and eternal life.

The picture that Paul gives in Colossians 1:18 is that Jesus is
the head of the body, which is the church, and He is the firstborn
from the dead. If we picture resurrection as a birth, then we can
apply to it the same order that applies to the natural birth of a
child from his mother's womb. As we all know, in a natural birth
the head comes out first and then the body follows. This applies
to the resurrection of Jesus and to our resurrection. Jesus, the
head, has come out in resurrection and this guarantees that we,
who are the body, will follow the head. It is a beautiful picture.
The resurrection of Jesus is our guarantee that we, who are united
to Him by faith, will also be resurrected as He was. He, the head,

has already come forth. We, the body, will follow in God's due season. Jesus Himself sums this up very succinctly: "Because I live, you will live also" (John 14:19).

His life is our life. We have a guarantee that we will share in His resurrection because we are united to Him.

OUR GOAL

The third fact about the resurrection is that it is the goal of our Christian living. Probably all of us would agree that we are not more committed to the Lord than Paul was. He was an apostle, he had seen the Lord, he had gifts of the Holy Spirit operating in his life, and he had preached and seen wonderful results. We might think that such a person would obviously be a candidate for the resurrection. But Paul did not think so, and his example is worth studying:

> Yet indeed I also count all things loss for the excellence of the knowledge of Christ Jesus my Lord, for whom I have suffered the loss of all things, and count them as rubbish, that I may gain Christ and be found in Him, not having my own righteousness, which is from the law, but that which is through faith in Christ, the righteousness which is from God by faith...
>
> Philippians 3:8–9

Your religious righteousness – your good acts, your church attendance and your prayers – are not sufficient. You must have a righteousness from God received by faith. That is God's own righteousness. Nothing else is good enough. You can be a very religious person, very regular in your church going, you can give generously to charity, but if you do not have God's righteousness, nothing else will get you into heaven. Paul was very concerned about this. He said, "That I may not trust in my own righteousness but have the righteousness that is from God through faith." Then he goes on in verse 10: "That I may know Him and the power of His resurrection, and the fellowship of His sufferings, being conformed to His death...."

I can certainly say, with Paul, that I want the power of Christ's resurrection. But what about the next phrase: the fellowship of His sufferings? By God's grace, I have come to a point where I actually do desire the fellowship of His sufferings. I would rather suffer with Jesus than be exempted from suffering and cut off from Jesus.

In World War II, I served as a Nursing Orderly in the British Royal Army Medical Corps, and sometimes I had to deal with soldiers who had been through battle conditions. I came to see that when men go through a really tough time together, they are bonded to one another in a way that nothing can break – even though they may be very unlike one another in many ways, socially, intellectually or economically. I think that is why Paul said *that I might know Him and the fellowship of His sufferings.* He wanted to be bonded with Jesus in a way that nothing could break.

One conclusion is clear: Nobody has the right to take it for granted that he will partake of the first resurrection. It is a goal that we have to aim at continually. In this Paul is our example:

> Not that I have already attained, or am already perfected; but I press on, that I may lay hold of that for which Christ Jesus has also laid hold of me. Brethren, I do not count myself to have apprehended; but one thing I do, forgetting those things which are behind and reaching forward to those things which are ahead, I press toward the goal for the prize of the upward call of God in Christ Jesus.

> verses 12–14

That was Paul's attitude toward attaining to the resurrection of the dead. He was a mature apostle with a record of tremendous successes. Still, he did not consider that he had already attained the resurrection of the dead, but his purpose was to attain it, and he said, in effect, "Nothing is going to stand between me and the fulfillment of Christ's purpose for me. I'm going to press toward that mark. I'm going to press onward and upward, and nothing is going` to hold me back. The things of time – human attitudes and personalities, situations in the world – none of them will deflect me from my supreme ambition, which is to attain to the resurrection from the dead."

How can our attitude be any different? How can we assume something that Paul could not assume? We should each cultivate this same attitude as Paul – to press toward the goal, make it our purpose to attain it, and let nothing stand between us and the fulfillment of our purpose. I believe that is the challenge of the resurrection for each of us.

9

BEGOTTEN AGAIN

So far, we have established the scriptural and historical fact of Christ's resurrection. Now we will take a look at what is made available to us in the mercy and provision of God through Christ's resurrection.

The first such blessing is that we can be begotten again, or you might use the phrase "born again." In introducing this, I want to go back for a moment to the prophecy of Hosea that we examined in chapter six:

> After two days He will revive us;
> On the third day He will raise us up,
> That we may live in His sight.
>
> Hosea 6:2

That is a clear prediction of the resurrection to take place on the third day. But as I pointed out, Hosea does not speak in the singular but in the plural. He does not say, speaking in the person of Christ through the Holy Spirit, "He will revive *me*, or He will raise *me* up," but he speaks in the plural, "He will revive *us*, He will raise *us* up." So, by the prophetic insight of the Holy Spirit, the Scripture reveals that, as believers, we are included in the resurrection of Jesus. Jesus died our death that we may be identified with Him by baptism into His burial. And by being identified with Him in burial, we might then also share in His resurrection.

> But God, who is rich in mercy, because of His great love with which He loved us, even when we were dead in trespasses, made us alive together with Christ (by grace you have been saved), and raised us up together, and made us sit together in the heavenly places in Christ Jesus.
>
> Ephesians 2:4–6

Remember, the word "together" in this passage occurs three times, each time indicating some experience that we share with Jesus through our faith in His atoning death. *God made us alive together with Christ, God raised us up together, and God made us sit together (or enthroned us) with Christ.* Paul speaks of all of these experiences in the past tense. In the eternal counsel of God, he is not describing something that is going to happen in the future but something that has already taken place. All that is required of us is that we enter into it by faith.

THE LAST ADAM, THE SECOND MAN

There is a very significant passage in that great resurrection chapter that we have looked at so many times, 1 Corinthians 15. Paul contrasts the old creation and the new creation – that which was opened up by the death and resurrection of Jesus Christ.

> And so it is written, "The first man Adam became a living being [or a living soul]." The last Adam became a life-giving

spirit. The first man was of the earth, made of dust; the second Man is the Lord from heaven.

1 Corinthians 15:45, 47

Paul here gives Jesus two titles: "the last Adam" and "the second Man." We need to set these two titles side by side, but in their right order. First, Jesus was the last Adam; second, He was the second Man. As the last Adam, He exhausted the entire evil inheritance that had come upon the whole Adamic race through sin and rebellion. It all came to its conclusion and climax, it was all exhausted, in the death of Jesus.

Then, when Jesus rose from the dead three days later as the second Man, He was the head of a new race. As the last Adam, He took upon Himself the entire evil inheritance resulting from Adam's rebellion, and sealed it off by death. Then as the second Man, He became the head of a new race of which all who believe become members.

The way by which we can enter into this new inheritance and become members of this new race in Christ is by being begotten again or born again. Both phrases are used, but I prefer the phrase "begotten again," because in correct English the word "beget" describes the father's part in procreation. It is God the Father who, through our faith in Jesus Christ, begets us again. But of course, the person who is begotten is also born again. So both phrases apply.

> Blessed be the God and Father of our Lord Jesus Christ, who according to His abundant mercy has begotten us again to a living hope through the resurrection of Jesus Christ from the dead.

1 Peter 1:3

By being identified by faith with Jesus in death, burial and resurrection, we pass with Him out of the old order – the old creation – into a new order, a new creation. We are begotten again by the power of God into this new race of which Jesus Christ is the Head. I call this the "Emmanuel Race" or the "God-with-us Race."

This was the purpose of the death and resurrection of Jesus. Once we are thus begotten again, or born again, Christ is from then on our inward source of eternal life. We have an entirely new source of life that is in Christ and is in heaven. The apostle Paul describes this:

> If then you then were raised with Christ [that is, identified with Him in resurrection], seek those things which are above, where Christ is, sitting at the right hand of God. Set your mind on things above, not on things on the earth. For you died [we died when Christ died – His death was our death], and your life is hidden with Christ in God. When Christ who is our life appears, then you also will appear with Him in glory.
>
> Colossians 3:1–4

Our inheritance is in the heavenlies, on the throne with Jesus. That is why we should set our minds on things above. That is very important advice, because the course of our lives is determined by that on which our minds are focused.

We died when Christ died; His death was our death. We have absolute security when we realize that our life is hidden with Christ in God.

Notice that tremendous phrase of limitless meaning: "Christ is our life." That life is absolutely inexhaustible. Every need is covered by the one fact that the resurrected, glorified, victorious

Christ is our life. Nothing can conquer that life. Nothing can overcome it. It is undefeatable, indestructible, and eternal.

In 2 Corinthians 4:16 Paul applies this to his experience, and it applies also to ours: "Therefore we do not lose heart. Even though our outward man is perishing, yet the inward man is being renewed day by day."

That beautiful message of encouragement tells us that we do not need to lose heart. Things may seem to be difficult or going against us outwardly, but Paul says we are connected to Jesus. By faith through the Holy Spirit, we have an inward source of life, and we are being continually renewed by this life within us, which is the resurrected, glorified Christ. Take time to meditate on those four pregnant words: "Christ is our life."

10

JUSTIFIED

Another tremendous revelation of the complete work of the cross is that through Christ's resurrection we can be justified, made completely righteous. The verb *justified* and the noun *justification* occur many times in the New Testament. They are important words, but I believe many Christians do not really understand the fullness of their meaning. So I will seek to give a clearer picture of what it is to be justified.

ABRAHAM: OUR EXAMPLE

The forefather of our faith, Abraham, provides the great example for us of being justified by faith. Paul speaks about the example and pattern of Abraham's faith and then shows how it applies to us:

> Yet he did not waver through unbelief regarding the promise of God, but was strengthened in his faith [or was made strong by his faith] and gave glory to God, being fully persuaded that God had power to do what he had promised.
>
> Romans 4:20–21, NIV

Abraham was fully persuaded that God had power to do what He had promised. How about you? Are you fully persuaded that God has power to do what He has promised? Paul then goes on to quote what the book of Genesis says about Abraham:

> This is why "it was credited to him as righteousness." The words, "it was credited to him" were written not for him alone, but also for us, to whom God will credit righteousness – for us who believe in him who raised Jesus our Lord from the dead. He [Jesus] was delivered over to death for our sins and was raised to life for our justification.
>
> verses 22–25, NIV

Paul applies the example of Abraham to us as believers in the New Covenant. If we believe with the same kind of faith Abraham had, then it will be credited to us for righteousness just as it was to Abraham. The last phrase states, "[Jesus] was raised to life [or resurrected] for our justification" – that is, that we might be made righteous, or that righteousness might be credited to us.

Abraham is an example of continuing to believe God's promise in spite of all discouragement or negative appearances. We, as Christians, must exercise the same kind of faith concerning Christ's death and resurrection.

There are two aspects to this transaction. First, by His death Christ paid the full and final penalty for our sins. So God's justice was satisfied by the death of Jesus on our behalf. God is not compromising His justice when He forgives our sins, because Jesus has paid the full penalty as our accepted legal representative.

OUR ACQUITTAL

The second aspect of this transaction comes out of Christ's resurrection. By His resurrection, Christ provided complete righteousness. We are acquitted of all guilt. We were justified – reckoned righteous. I want to emphasize the word *complete* – not partial, but complete. It is very important to see that our acquittal depends on Christ's resurrection. Paul brings this home in 1 Corinthians 15:17: "And if Christ is not risen, your faith is futile; and you are still in your sins!"

So our acquittal depends on the resurrection of Jesus. When God resurrected Jesus, He also vindicated Him. Two human courts had previously condemned Him to death – both the secular court of Rome and the religious court of the Jewish Sanhedrin. By resurrection, God reversed those unjust verdicts and vindicated the righteousness of Jesus. But when His righteousness was vindicated by resurrection, vindication was extended to all who would be identified with Him in His resurrection. This is clearly stated in 2 Corinthians 5:21: "For He [God] made him [Jesus] who knew no sin to be sin for us, that we might become the righteousness of God in Him."

Jesus was made sin with our sinfulness and paid the full penalty for our sin, that we, in turn, through faith, might be identified with His righteousness, which was vindicated by resurrection. By this, we are justified, made completely righteous, because the righteousness that is reckoned to me through Christ's resurrection is a righteousness that never knew sin. And that is the only righteousness that will ever be accepted in heaven.

THE HEART AND THE MOUTH

Because it took Christ's resurrection to insure our acquittal and justification, there are, therefore, two logical requirements for us to enter into salvation. The first concerns the heart, the second concerns the mouth. Paul describes the righteousness of the heart in Romans 10:

> But the righteousness of faith speaks in this way, "Do not say in your heart, 'Who will ascend into heaven?'" (that is, to bring Christ down from above) or, "'Who will descend into the abyss?'" (that is, to bring Christ up from the dead).
>
> Romans 10:6–7

Paul is saying the righteousness of faith does not have to do what Christ has already done on our behalf. We have to begin by affirming in our hearts that we accept what Christ has already done it for us.

So the first requirement is that we have to believe in the heart that God raised Jesus from the dead. But that is not sufficient. The second requirement concerns the mouth. We have to confess with our mouths Jesus as Lord. We have to acknowledge His Lordship, not just His Lordship in general over the universe, but His Lordship in particular over our own lives. There has to be a surrendering of our wills, a surrendering of ourselves, an act of commitment to the Lordship of Jesus. In Romans 10:8–10 Paul explains that our commitment is not complete until it is verbalized:

> But what does it say? "The word is near you, even in your mouth and in your heart" (that is, the word of faith which we preach): that if you confess with your mouth the Lord Jesus [or Jesus as Lord] and believe in your heart that God has raised Him from the dead, you will be saved. For with the heart one believes to righteousness, and with the mouth confession is made unto salvation.

Some people believe in the heart, but they have never verbalized their commitment with their mouth. If you are one of those, I want to recommend to you that you take the second step. Perhaps you already believe in your heart that God raised Jesus from the dead. Maybe you have confessed it many times in church. But have you totally committed yourself to His Lordship, and have you acknowledged Him as Lord with your mouth? There has to be an individual, public confession of what we believe in our heart. That is the key to entering into salvation. Believe with the heart that God resurrected Jesus, confess with your mouth Jesus as Lord. If you do that, the Scripture says, "You will be saved."

11

Victory Over All Enemies

Christ's victory assures our victory over all our enemies, particularly over death. Any religion that does not have a satisfactory answer to death cannot meet humanity's deepest needs. I believe Christianity is the only religion that does have that answer, and it is because of Christ's resurrection.

The Resurrected Victor

A glorious picture of Christ as the resurrected victor is found in the book of Revelation. This is how Jesus appeared to the apostle John on the Isle of Patmos after His resurrection and ascension:

> I was in the Spirit on the Lord's Day, and I heard behind me a loud voice as of a trumpet, saying, "I am the Alpha and the Omega, the First and the Last."... Then I turned to see the voice that spoke with me. And having turned I saw seven golden lampstands, and in the midst of the seven lampstands One like the Son of Man, clothed with a garment down to the feet and girded about the chest with a golden

band. His head and His hair were white like wool, as white as snow, and His eyes like a flame of fire; His feet were like fine brass, as if refined in a furnace, and His voice as the sound of many waters; He had in His right hand seven stars, out of His mouth went a sharp two-edged sword, and His countenance was like the sun shining in its strength. And when I saw Him, I fell at His feet as dead. But He laid His right hand on me saying to me, "Do not be afraid; I am the First and the Last. I am He who lives, and was dead, and behold, I am alive forevermore. Amen. And I have the keys of Hades and of Death."

Revelation 1:10–18

Isn't that a glorious picture? That is our representative, our Head, the One who died for us and who paid the penalty for our sins. But thank God, He did not remain dead. He did not remain in the tomb. He was resurrected and He was raised up to the Father's right hand, to the throne. There He received the glory as the only begotten Son of God, the glory of the Victor, the glory of the Ruler. There is so much glory in that description of the resurrected Christ: "His feet were like fine brass, as if refined in a furnace . . . His voice as the sound of many waters . . . His head and His hair were white like wool . . . His eyes like a flame of fire . . . out of His mouth went a sharp two-edged sword."

It is very significant that before the resurrection of Jesus, John the apostle actually rested his head on Jesus' chest. He came that close to Him. But when the power of the resurrected, glorified Christ came upon Him, it totally overcame John. He became like one dead. That reveals the measure of the power and the glory that there is in the resurrected Christ.

DEATH AND HADES

Particularly I want to emphasize the words of Jesus in verse 18: "I am He who lives, and was dead, and behold, I am alive forevermore. Amen. *And I have the keys of Hades and of Death*" (*emphasis added*).

Let me explain a little about Hades and Death. First of all, death is not merely a physical condition. It is not merely the separation of life from the body. Both Death and Hades are evil angels, Satan's representatives, ruling over a kingdom of darkness. This is so clearly pictured in a further section of the revelation granted to John there on the Isle of Patmos.

> So I looked, and behold, a pale horse. And the name of him who sat on it was Death, and Hades followed with him. And power was given to them over a fourth of the earth, to kill with sword, with hunger, with death, and by the beasts of the earth.
>
> Revelation 6:8

We see then that both Death and Hades are persons, satanic angels, representing Satan, administrators of his evil kingdom of darkness. Death claims men's bodies; Hades claims their souls. Between His death and resurrection Jesus descended into their realm. He stripped them of their authority, and He took away their keys from them. When He appeared to John, He said, "I have the keys of Death and of Hades." Oh, how real that is and how important for every one of us to know that Jesus holds those keys!

We need to know that death is already defeated, but not yet destroyed. Paul tells us in 1 Corinthians 15:25–26: "For He must reign till He has put all enemies under His feet. The last enemy that will be destroyed is death."

So death is defeated but not yet destroyed. In the meanwhile, however, Jesus has already taken the sting from death.

> For this corruptible must put on incorruption, and this mortal must put on immortality. So when this corruptible has put on incorruption, and this mortal has put on immortality, then shall be brought to pass the saying that is written: "Death is swallowed up in victory" [Christ's victory has swallowed up death.]. "O Death, where is your sting? O Hades, where is your victory?" The sting of death is sin, and the strength of sin is the law. But thanks be to God, who gives us the victory through our Lord Jesus Christ.
>
> verses 53–57

Jesus has taken away the victory from death. By His victory Jesus has also taken away the sting from death. Death is now a servant of God's purposes, a defeated enemy waiting to be destroyed. In Romans 8, Paul returns to this theme with some beautiful words:

> Who shall separate us from the love of Christ? Shall tribulation, or distress, or persecution, or famine, or nakedness, or peril, or sword? As it is written: "For Your sake we are killed all day long; we are accounted as sheep for the slaughter." Yet in all these things we are more than conquerors through Him who loved us. For I am persuaded that neither death nor life, nor angels nor principalities nor powers, nor things present nor things to come, nor height nor depth, nor any other created thing, shall be able to separate us from the love of God which is in Christ Jesus our Lord.
>
> Romans 8:35–39

All of that is obtained for us through the resurrection. Paul tells us that "Christ is our life." The resurrected, glorified Christ is our life. Nothing can touch that life. Nothing can destroy it. It is indestructible and totally victorious.

In the light of Christ's victory over death, I want to point you now to some promises that Jesus gave in anticipation of His victory. When He uses the phrase "most assuredly," it introduces a statement that is absolutely authoritative.

> Most assuredly, I say to you, he who hears My word and believes in Him who sent Me has everlasting life, and shall not come into judgment, but has passed from death into life.
>
> John 5:24

Notice that this is stated in the past tense. It is not something that is going to happen in the future. When we believe in the death and resurrection of Jesus Christ, by our faith, we have already passed from death into life. Death has no more dominion over us. Death has no more claims over us. Death is merely the gateway into a new life. In John 8:51–52 we have this assurance from Jesus Himself: "Most assuredly, I say to you, if anyone keeps My word he shall never see death.... If anyone keeps My word he shall never taste death."

Can you believe that? It is a promise from the lips of Jesus. He does not say that we will never experience physical death, but He says that those two evil angels, Death and Hades who follows behind him, have no more claims on us. They are excluded by the name and the blood of Jesus. So when death becomes our portion, we are not going *down* into another world, into a kingdom of darkness, but we are going *up* into the very presence of

God. This is guaranteed for us by the death and resurrection of Jesus on our behalf.

That is how it was with Stephen as he was facing martyrdom:

> "Look!" [he cried] "I see the heavens opened and the Son of Man standing at the right hand of God!" [And then a little further on, as he was being stoned, he said:] "Lord Jesus, receive my spirit." Then he knelt down and cried out with a loud voice, "Lord, do not charge them with this sin." And when he had said this, he fell asleep.
>
> Acts 7:56, 59–60

We need to bear in mind that Scripture is very careful about the words it uses. As a rule it does not speak about believers dying. It speaks about them "falling asleep." For them death is only a temporary sleep out of which they will be awakened on the resurrection morning.

12

THE FIRST RESURRECTION

There is yet one more blessing that is made available to us through Christ's resurrection. His resurrection is the guarantee of our resurrection. This follows from the statement found in Colossians 1:18: "And He is the head of the body, the church, who is the beginning, the firstborn from the dead, that in all things He may have the preeminence."

In chapter eight, "What the Resurrection Means for Us," we looked at this Scripture, which compares the resurrection of Jesus to the birth of a baby. We may now take this one step further: when the head of the baby emerges, we know that the body will follow. In like manner, since Jesus, the Head, has been resurrected, this guarantees that the body (the Church) will follow.

FIRSTBORN FROM THE DEAD

Now let us look at the greeting with which John prefaces his message to the churches:

> John, to the seven churches which are in Asia: Grace to you and peace from Him who is and who was and who is to come [that is, God the Father], and from the seven Spirits who are

before His throne [the Holy Spirit in His seven aspects], and from Jesus Christ, the faithful witness, the firstborn from the dead, and the ruler over the kings of the earth.

Revelation 1:4–5

There are three statements made there about Jesus that follow one another in logical order. First, He is the faithful witness, the one who faithfully and completely represented the Father to the people of His time. He never compromised, never spoke a false word, and never misrepresented God. Even at the cost of His own life He remained the faithful witness. Because He was the faithful witness, therefore He became the firstborn from the dead, or the first to be resurrected from the dead. And as the firstborn from the dead, He then became the ruler over the kings of the earth. Resurrection leads to rulership. Again, the use of the word "firstborn" indicates that there are others to follow. Christ was resurrected to rule, and so shall we be.

I have quoted several times from Ephesians 2 the three "together" statements of Paul: we are made alive together, we are resurrected together, and we are enthroned together. Resurrection leads to the throne! Paul brings out the same truth in 2 Timothy 2:11–12, where he is quoting what is apparently a saying that was current in the early church: "This is a faithful saying: For if we died with Him [Jesus] we shall also live with Him. If we endure, we shall also reign with Him."

As we have seen, if we are identified with Jesus in death, we shall be identified with Him in resurrection. If we hold faithfully in our witness as He held in His witness, we shall be like Him, resurrected to reign with Him. This is the amazing promise of Revelation 3:21: "To him who overcomes I [Jesus] will grant to sit with Me on My throne, as I also overcame and sat down with My Father on His throne."

That is a breathtaking promise! Jesus overcame and the Father raised Him to the throne to rule with Him. Now Jesus says, "Through My death and resurrection, you can overcome. And if you overcome, I will do for you what My Father did for Me. I will raise you up, and I will seat you with Me on My throne to rule."

Resurrection in Three Stages

In 1 Corinthians 15:22–24 Paul outlines the order of resurrection, and he indicates that there will be three successive phases:

> For as in Adam all die, even so in Christ all shall be made alive. [In due course all will be resurrected.] But each one in his own order: Christ the firstfruits, afterward those who are Christ's at His coming. Then comes the end, when He delivers the kingdom to God the Father, when He puts an end to all rule and all authority and power.

So we see the order of resurrection. Christ the firstfruits – that has already taken place. The next phase is "those who are Christ's at His coming." This is called in Scripture "the first resurrection." When Jesus returns, these believers will be caught up to meet Him in the air and will be with Him forever. The Scripture comments, "Blessed and holy is he who has part in the first resurrection" (Revelation 20:6). Then comes the end, the final resurrection of all the remaining dead who are called forth to appear before God and answer for the lives that they have led. This is described at the end of Revelation 20.

How can we qualify for the first resurrection? This is a most important and practical question. It is important for every person to know the answer, which is given in verse 23: "But each man in his own order: Christ the firstfruits, afterward *those who are Christ's* at His coming." (*emphasis added*).

That sums it up. You can qualify for the first resurrection by belonging to Jesus Christ. Jesus loves you, but He is a jealous lover. Many times the Bible tells us God is jealous. I used to think that was one of God's weaknesses, but over the years I have come to see that it is a mark of His love. Is it not amazing that the Creator should be jealous over a little piece of clay into which He has breathed His Spirit?

Jesus is a jealous lover. He wants you for His own, but He will not share you with anybody else. He will not share you with the world, and He will not share you with the devil. So if you are going to take part in the first resurrection, you need to know that it will only be because you belong unreservedly to Jesus Christ. This first resurrection is only for those who are Christ's – not *almost* Christ's or *partially* Christ's, but totally Christ's. That is the basic requirement.

Ask yourself now: "Do I really belong to Jesus Christ, unreservedly and totally? Or are there areas in my life that are not surrendered to Him? Are there areas in my life where some other claim has been asserted or something else is demanding my affection, my attention?" If so, you will have to change and put things right. You will have to make a total commitment to Jesus. That is the first requirement.

JACOB LOVED, ESAU HATED

As I was meditating on this, I thought about a very remarkable statement that the Lord makes in Malachi 1:2–3: "Jacob I have loved, but Esau I have hated."

God is a Person with strong feelings. He loves, and He also hates. But why did God love Jacob? In many ways he was not a very lovable character. However, Jacob had one thing that commended him to God. He really wanted God's best. Sometimes he went in rather crooked ways to get it, but his priorities were right. He wanted the birthright, the blessing of his father Isaac.

On the other hand, Esau, who should have had the birthright, was indifferent toward it. After a hunting excursion, he came back and there was Jacob with a pot of lentil soup. I know from my own experience in the Middle East that when lentil soup is being prepared, the aroma permeates the house, and the only thing you can think about is lentil soup.

So here comes Esau in from a long hunting trip, very hungry, and he smells this lentil soup. Jacob stands there saying, "I'll give you some. All you have to do is sell me your birthright." Esau thinks, "What good is my birthright when I'm hungry. All I need is something to eat." So he makes a bargain with Jacob.

God hates an attitude that does not appreciate the birthright. He hates an attitude that will take a fleshly desire and put it ahead of His birthright.

For you it could be many things – for instance, food. Some people are enslaved by food; it is the most important thing in their life. It is the thing they talk and think about most, and it is the thing they spend a lot of money on. There are other desires as well – such as alcohol, sex or money – that capture people through their appetites. But anything that takes precedence over God's birthright in your life is hateful to God. If there is such a thing in your life, you need to take it to the cross.

As we think about this glorious theme of resurrection, it is very natural for us to ask ourselves, "What will the resurrection be like?" This question is actually asked in the New Testament and answered in various places. I'll explore this in chapter fifteen, "The Nature of Our Resurrection Bodies." But first, let us look at what happens when a person dies.

13

What Comes After Death?

I want to draw aside just a corner of the veil that separates this world from the next by giving you a glimpse of what comes after death.

Before the Death of Jesus

We need to understand that the death and the resurrection of Jesus were cosmic in their effects. They produced results that affected the entire universe. In particular, they produced profound and permanent changes in the unseen world and in the destiny that awaits the souls of righteous believers after they depart this life.

The best way to understand man's ongoing destiny – and his destiny after death – is to look at the method of man's creation as it is described for us in Genesis 2:7: "And the LORD God formed man of the dust of the ground, and breathed into his nostrils the breath of life; and man became a living being [or soul]."

We notice that for total human personality there are two distinct sources: the material part of man – his body – has its source in the earth. It comes from below. But the non-material part of man – his soul – has its source in God, and comes from above. So, man is a union of constituents from two different sources: physical from the earth below, and spiritual from God above. We must bear this in mind as we study man's ongoing destiny.

At death, these two constituent parts of man are again separated. The body returns to the earth from which it came and there decays; the soul passes into the unseen world. There are two words in the Bible for this unseen world. In Hebrew it is called *Sheol*, and in the Greek of the New Testament it is called *Hades*.

We will examine a picture from the Old Testament of souls in Sheol. It is a prediction of God's judgment on the king of Babylon, and it describes how the soul of the king of Babylon descends into Sheol, and how his soul is recognized there and, in a sense, rated by other departed kings and persons who have died previously:

> Sheol from beneath is excited over you to meet you
>> when you come;
> It arouses for you the spirits of the dead, all the leaders
>> of the earth;
> It raises all the kings of the nations from their
>> thrones.
> They will all respond and say to you,
> "Even you have been made weak as we,
> You have become like us."
>
> Isaiah 14:9–10, NAS

Sheol is not the ultimate destiny of departed souls, but a place of temporary imprisonment awaiting final resurrection and judgment. Later on we will see a description of this.

In Ezekiel 32:18–32, there is a similar picture of God's judgment on Pharaoh, king of Egypt, and on many other Gentile kings and their armies who had been slain in battle:

> "Son of man, wail for the multitude of Egypt, and bring it down, her and the daughters of the powerful nations, to the nether world, with those who go down to the pit;
>
> 'Whom do you surpass in beauty?
>
> Go down and make your bed with the uncircumcised.'...
>
> Assyria is there and all her company; her graves are round about her....
>
> Elam is there and all her multitude around her grave; all of them slain, fallen by the sword, who went down uncircumcised to the lower parts of the earth....
>
> Meshech, Tubal and all their multitude are there; their graves surround them. All of them were slain by the sword uncircumcised, though they instilled their terror in the land of the living....
>
> There also is Edom, its kings, and all its princes, who for all their might are laid with those slain by the sword; they will lie with the uncircumcised, and with those who go down to the pit.
>
> There also are the chiefs of the north, all of them, and all the Sidonians, who in spite of the terror resulting from their might, in shame went down with the slain. So they lay down uncircumcised with those slain by the sword, and bore their disgrace with those who go down to the pit.
>
> These Pharaoh will see, and he will be comforted for all his multitude slain by the sword, even Pharaoh and all his army," declares the Lord God. "Though I instilled a terror of him in

the land of the living, yet he will be made to lie down among the uncircumcised along with those slain by the sword, even Pharaoh and all his multitude," declares the Lord God.

Ezekiel 32:18–19, 22, 24, 26, 30–32, NAS

There are several features that are common to both of these passages:

1. There is no indication that those departed souls had any knowledge of current events on earth.
2. However, they did have a recollection of their previous conditions on earth.
3. There is a definite persistence of personality.
4. There is recognition of one person by another.
5. There is communication between one person and another.
6. There is an awareness of the present conditions in Sheol.
7. There is correspondence between the state of departed souls as they were on earth and their state in Sheol, in the sense that kings on earth were still recognized as kings in Sheol.

In the New Testament we have a picture given by Jesus Himself of what happens to souls that depart this life. This is the story of a beggar named Lazarus and a rich man:

There was a certain rich man who was clothed in purple and fine linen and fared sumptuously every day. But there was a certain beggar named Lazarus, full of sores, who was laid at his gate, desiring to be fed with the crumbs which fell from the rich man's table. Moreover the dogs came and licked his sores. So it was that the beggar died, and was carried by the angels to Abraham's bosom. The rich man also died and was buried. And being in torments in Hades, he lifted up his eyes and saw Abraham afar off, and Lazarus in his bosom. Then he cried and said, "Father Abraham, have mercy on me, and send Lazarus that he may dip the tip of his finger in water and cool my tongue; for I am tormented in the flame." But Abraham said, "Son, remember that in your lifetime you received your good things, and likewise Lazarus evil things; but now he is comforted and you are tormented. And besides all this, between us and you there is a great gulf fixed, so that those who want to pass from here to you cannot, nor can those from there pass to us."

Luke 16:19–26

Now remember that these are the words of Jesus Himself – the most reliable of all authorities – and remember also that nowhere is it stated that this is a parable. It is a record of actual events that took place in the period before the death and resurrection of Jesus.

Jesus' account repeats many features from the Old Testament. First, we notice that the body returns to the earth, but the soul passes out into the unseen world – in the New Testament called Hades. In this unseen world, there are the following features, all of which are carried over from the account in the Old Testament:

First, there is a recollection of previous conditions on earth. Abraham actually said to the rich man, "*Remember* that in your lifetime you received your good things" – so clearly, there is remembrance of previous conditions on earth.

Second, there is a persistence of personality. Lazarus was still Lazarus; Abraham was still Abraham; the rich man was still the rich man, though no longer rich.

Third, there was recognition of one person by another. The rich man recognized both Abraham and Lazarus.

Fourth, there was a consciousness of present conditions. Particularly, the rich man was very conscious of the agony and the torment in which he found himself.

However, there is one important extra feature that is added in this account by Jesus: there is a complete separation between the righteous and the unrighteous. Though both are in this place reserved for the souls of the departed, they are in completely different sections of that place, and there is a great difference between what is happening to them. The wicked rich man is in torment – he is being tormented in flame. But the righteous poor man is in a place of rest that is described as Abraham's bosom. The mention of Abraham particularly indicates that it is for those who follow in the steps of Abraham's faith.

One other important feature is included in the account given by Jesus: God's angels took charge of the soul of Lazarus. Angels carried him to his place of rest. We find also that this corresponds to the experience of the wicked: Satan's angels took charge of their souls. This is described in Revelation 6:8:

> I looked, and there before me was a pale horse! Its rider was named Death, and Hades was following close behind him. They were given power over a fourth of the earth to kill by sword, famine and plague, and by the wild beasts of the earth.

We see there that both Death and Hades are persons. They are, in fact, satanic angels. It is usually taught that Death has power over men's bodies, and Hades has power over men's souls. Death causes men to die; Hades, who follows behind him, takes charge of the souls who have died in sin and carries them away into the place of imprisonment and torment that is appointed for them. So, we see in these passages, both from the Old and the New Testaments, a consistent picture of the destiny of departed souls during the period prior to the death and resurrection of Jesus.

AFTER THE DEATH OF JESUS

While Jesus' body lay in the tomb, His soul descended into Hades and, as a result, certain important and permanent changes took place. The record of these events is found primarily in the first epistle of Peter. We need to look at two distinct statements. First, 1 Peter 3:18–20:

> For Christ also died for sins once for all, the just for the unjust, in order that He might bring us to God, having been put to death in the flesh, but made alive in the spirit; in which also He went and made proclamation to the spirits now in prison, who once were disobedient, when the patience of God kept waiting in the days of Noah, during the construction of the ark, in which a few, that is, eight persons, were brought safely through the water.

> NAS

This reveals Christ in the spirit – but not in His body – descending into Hades; and it describes how He made a proclamation to the spirits of unrighteous persons who were there in prison. The particular persons specified were those who had been disobedient to God and had broken God's laws in the days of Noah.

The second distinct statement is found in 1 Peter 4:6: "For

the gospel has for this purpose been preached even to those who are dead, that though they are judged in the flesh as men, they may live in the spirit according to the will of God" (NAS).

This is not the same as the previous statement, there is an important distinction: different words are used in the Greek. In the first passage, it says that Jesus made a proclamation, but in the second passage it says that the gospel was preached. "The gospel," of course, is the good news that always centers in the death and resurrection of Jesus.

What was the difference between the two? And what exactly happened? Let us look first at what happened to the righteous believers in Abraham's bosom. To them, Jesus brought good news – the gospel. The good news was this: Jesus' death and His shed blood had paid the price for sin. Consequently, God was now prepared to give them complete pardon and to release them from this place of waiting. Their bodies had suffered sin's penalty, which was death, but their souls received God's pardon through their faith in Jesus.

Now, let us look at what happened to the unrighteous in this prison. Jesus made to them a proclamation. So far as I know, there is no passage in the Bible that tells us what this proclamation was. I like to phrase Jesus' proclamation in terms such as this: "This place is now under new management!" Why do I say that? Look at what Jesus said to John on the island of Patmos when He appeared to him in His glory:

> And when I saw Him, I fell at His feet as dead. But He laid His right hand on me, saying to me, "Do not be afraid; I am the First and the Last. I am He who lives, and was dead, and behold, I am alive forevermore. Amen. *And I have the keys of Hades and of Death.*"
>
> Revelation 1:17–18 (*emphasis added*)

By His death and His propitiatory sacrifice, Jesus had earned the right to wrest from the hand of those two satanic angels, Death and Hades, the keys to that place of imprisonment. Consequently, from then on, Jesus had the right to liberate those who had been pardoned. This He did, then, when He ascended out of Hades and then ascended right into heaven. He took with Him the liberated souls from Abraham's bosom:

> Therefore it says,
>   "When He [Jesus] ascended on high,
>   He led captive a host of captives,
>   And He gave gifts to men."
>   (Now this expression, "He ascended," what does it mean except that He also had descended into the lower parts of the earth? He who descended is Himself also He who ascended far above all the heavens, that He might fill all things.)
>   Ephesians 4:8–10, NAS

This Scripture tells us that those believers who had been the captives of Hades became Jesus' captives through His atoning sacrifice and through the price that He paid of His shed blood. He obtained the rights to release those captives and take them with Him when He ascended on high. So after descending to the lower part of the earth and bringing the good news of redemption to the captives in Abraham's bosom, Jesus released them using the keys of Death and of Hades, which He had received. Then, when He ascended into the heaven of God's presence, He took them out with Him. He led captive a host of captives.

This is also described in Matthew where it speaks about the death of Jesus on the cross and the events that followed:

> Then, behold, the veil of the temple was torn in two from top to bottom; and the earth quaked, and the rocks were

split, and the graves were opened; and many bodies of the saints who had fallen asleep were raised [that is the first resurrection of believers that is recorded], and coming out of the graves after His resurrection, they went into the holy city and appeared to many.

Matthew 27:51–53

This is speaking about the host of captives whom Jesus liberated. In Hebrews 11:40 we are told about the Old Testament saints as compared to the New Testament saints: "God having provided something better for us [that is, the saints of the New Testament] that they [the Old Testament saints] should not be made perfect apart from us." Only after the death and resurrection of Jesus could the Old Testament saints enter into that which they had been believing and trusting for and waiting to see accomplished. It was fulfilled when Jesus came down into their place of imprisonment and released them and took them with Him.

As a result of the death and resurrection of Jesus, and the events that we have been examining, the entire situation for righteous believers since that time has been radically changed. From that moment on, righteous believers no longer descend into a place of waiting or imprisonment after death, but have direct access to the presence of God in heaven.

The first clear example of this is provided by the first martyr, Stephen, whose martyrdom is described in Acts 7:55–56, 59–60:

But he, being full of the Holy Spirit, gazed into heaven and saw the glory of God, and Jesus standing at the right hand of God, and said, "Look! I see the heavens opened and the Son of Man standing at the right hand of God!" ... And they stoned Stephen as he was calling on God and saying, "Lord Jesus, receive my spirit." Then he knelt down and cried out with a loud voice, "Lord, do not charge them with this sin." And when he had said this, he fell asleep.

Just before his death, Stephen had a clear vision into the heavenly regions in the world beyond. He saw the glory of God and Jesus standing at the right hand of God, and he knew that was where he was going. His prayer was, "Receive my spirit." He did not go down into Sheol or to Hades, but his spirit was taken straight up into the presence of the Lord.

Then we can look in 2 Corinthians at the testimony of Paul:

> So we are always confident, knowing that while we are at home in the body we are absent from the Lord.... We are confident, yes, well pleased rather to be absent from the body and to be present with the Lord.

> 2 Corinthians 5:6, 8

For Paul there were two alternatives. As long as he was at home in the body, he was absent from the Lord, but at the moment that he became absent from the body, he would be present with the Lord. There was no question of his going down into Sheol or Hades.

> For to me, to live is Christ, and to die is gain. But if I live on in the flesh, this will mean fruit from my labor; yet what I shall choose I cannot tell. For I am hard-pressed between the two, having a desire to depart and be with Christ, which is far better. Nevertheless to remain in the flesh is more needful for you.

> Philippians 1:21–24

Here again we find that Paul saw two clear alternatives set before him. The one was to remain living in the flesh, which would benefit the Christians amongst whom he was working. The other, which he himself preferred, was to depart and to be with Christ.

The death of Jesus Christ on the cross and the shed blood that purchased our redemption had radically changed the destiny of righteous believers. It was no longer a question of going down into Sheol and waiting there in Abraham's bosom for the hour of release and redemption.

The spirits of true believers – through faith in Jesus – having been made righteous with His righteousness and redeemed with His blood, have immediate access into the heavenlies. It is indicated in the book of Revelation that there is a paradise, a garden of rest in the heavenlies, to which these righteous souls have access (see Revelation 14:13).

It is appropriate to conclude this chapter with the following passage from 1 Corinthians 15:55: "O Death, where is your sting? O Hades, where is your victory?"

The death and resurrection of Jesus robbed Death of its sting and Hades of its victory. How thankful we should be to God for all that has been purchased for us by the death of Jesus.

14

THE RESURRECTION OF BELIEVERS

In the New Testament, the resurrection of righteous believers is always closely associated with the second coming of Christ. The Greek word *parousia* is normally used for this second coming. *Parousia* means literally "presence."

There are many different prophecies in the Bible relating to this event – there are also many different interpretations of exactly what is going to take place at the return of Jesus. For my part, I offer one simple expression of opinion. It seems to me – on the basis of the meaning of the word *parousia* – that it need not necessarily describe one single, brief event, but it could apply to a series of events that follow one another in quick succession.

Rather than go into the controversial aspects of this subject, I would like to list five main purposes that the coming (or the return) of Jesus will fulfill. I certainly am not suggesting that they are the only purposes, nor am I necessarily suggesting that they will take place in this order:

1. Jesus will receive to Himself the church as His bride.
2. Israel as a nation will be saved.
3. Satan and the Antichrist will be overthrown.
4. The gentile nations will be judged.
5. Christ's millennial kingdom on earth will be established.

RESURRECTION OF THE RIGHTEOUS DEAD

As an integral part of all this, the resurrection of righteous believers will take place. This is described by Paul, and he indicates that he is speaking by revelation:

> But I do not want you to be ignorant, brethren, concerning those who have fallen asleep, lest you sorrow as others who have no hope. For if we believe that Jesus died and rose again, even so God will bring with Him those who sleep in Jesus [that is, those who have died in the faith]. For this we say to you by the word of the Lord, that we who are alive and remain until the coming of the Lord will be no means precede those who are asleep. For the Lord Himself will descend from heaven with a shout, with the voice of an archangel, and with the trumpet of God. And the dead in Christ will rise first. Then we who are alive and remain shall be caught up together with them in the clouds to meet the Lord in the air. And thus we shall always be with the Lord. Therefore comfort one another with these words.
>
> 1 Thessalonians 4:13–18

We need to bear in mind that these are words of comfort and to receive them in that way. They are not words of confusion.

Let's look once more at "The Resurrection of the Dead" section of *Foundational Truths For Christian Living* in which I have given the following outline of the event that Paul describes in 1 Thessalonians 4:

The primary purpose of Paul's teaching here is to comfort Christian believers concerning other Christians – relatives or other loved ones – who have died. These Christians who have died are described as "those who have fallen asleep"; or, more precisely, "those who sleep in Jesus." This means those who have died in the faith of the gospel. Paul's message of comfort is based on the assurance that these, and all other true believers, will be resurrected.

The actual picture that Paul gives of this phase of the resurrection is as follows.

First, there will be three dramatic sounds to herald it. The first sound will be the shout of the Lord Jesus Christ Himself, as He Himself had predicted:

> All who are in the graves will hear His voice and come forth – those who have done good, to the resurrection of life, and those who have done evil, to the resurrection of condemnation.

> JOHN 5:28–29

It is the voice of Christ alone that has power to call the dead out of their graves. However, at this particular moment He will call forth only the righteous dead – only those who have died in the faith. The calling forth of the unrighteous dead will be reserved for a later phase of resurrection.

The other two sounds that will be heard at this point will be the voice of the archangel and the trumpet of God. The archangel here referred to is probably Gabriel, since it appears to be his special ministry to proclaim upon earth impending interventions of God in the affairs of men.

All through the Bible, one main use of the trumpet is to gather the Lord's people together in any special time of crisis. The sound of the trumpet at this point will be the signal for all the Lord's people to gather together with Him as He descends from heaven to meet them.

Upon earth two great events will occur in swift succession. First, all true believers who have died in the faith will be resurrected. Second, all true believers alive on earth at that moment will undergo an instantaneous, supernatural change in their bodies.

Then both these companies of believers – those who were resurrected and those whose bodies were changed without dying – will together be swiftly raised by God's supernatural power from the earth up into the air. There they will be received into clouds, and within these clouds they will be reunited with their Lord and with each other. Thereafter the Lord and His redeemed believers will forever be united in unbroken harmony and fellowship.

pages 443–444

This same event is described again by Paul in 1 Corinthians:

Behold, I tell you a mystery: We shall not all sleep, but we shall all be changed – in a moment, in the twinkling of an eye, at the last trumpet. For the trumpet will sound, and the dead will be raised incorruptible, and we [who are still alive on earth at the time] shall be changed.

1 Corinthians 15:51–52

The word sleep is only used in the Scripture of those who die in the faith, because it speaks of an awakening. What a dramatic event that will be! I love that phrase, "in the twinkling of an eye." It means that at one moment you and I, as believers, will be looking at one another, seeing one another just as we always have. Then there will be a flash of brilliant light that will cause us to blink just for a moment; and when we open our eyes again, we will see one another as completely different. In just that split second, our physical bodies will have been totally transformed by the supernatural power of God, and we will have totally different kinds of bodies. That is the glorious hope that lies ahead of every true believer.

JESUS COMES AS A THIEF

In various places Jesus compares His coming again to that of a thief. In Revelation 16:15 He said: "Behold, I am coming as a thief...."

In Matthew 24:42–43 Jesus said:

> "Watch therefore, for you do not know what hour your Lord is coming. But know this, that if the master of the house had known what hour the thief would come, he would have watched and not have allowed his house to be broken into."

Here again, Jesus said that there is some correspondence between His coming again and the coming of a thief. This is in agreement with the phrase that was used by Paul in 1 Thessalonians 4:17 where he says, "We ... shall be caught up." The Greek verb is *harpazo*. It is also used in various other places in the New Testament. In Acts 8:39 we read, "The Spirit of the Lord snatched Philip away" (NAS). Philip suddenly disappeared out of the sight of the eunuch, whom he had just baptized, and the eunuch went on his way, but Philip was no longer to be seen anywhere. The translation there states he was "snatched away."

In John 10:12, speaking about the wolf coming in among the sheep, it says, "The wolf snatches them" (NAS), and it uses the same word, *harpazo*.

Matthew 13:19 uses the same word about the birds that catch away the seeds sown by the wayside, and it says, "The evil one comes and snatches away [the] ... seed" (NAS).

When Jude 23 speaks about snatching people out of the fire, it is the same word that is used in these other passages. I think that as we put the passages together, it gives us a rather vivid picture of what is going to take place when Jesus comes. The verb *harpazo*, "to snatch away," suggests one single, swift, intentional act. It is all going to be over very quickly. Just like the thief grabs something and runs with it, not stopping to look back for a moment, so Jesus will come and take His people to Himself.

There is one important difference, however, between what Jesus will do and what a thief does. The important difference is this: the thief takes that which does not belong to him, but Jesus is only going to take that which belongs to Him. First Corinthians 15:23, in speaking about this tremendous moment that lies ahead, confirms this. It says, "Those who are Christ's at His coming." Christ is coming only for those who are His own – only those who have been redeemed and are completely dedicated to Him, so that they no longer belong to themselves but to Christ. Are you one of those?

15

THE NATURE OF
OUR RESURRECTION
BODIES

In the last chapter, we looked at one of the main events associated with the second coming of Christ: the resurrection of righteous believers. Now we will take this topic one step further and learn about the new kind of body with which believers will be resurrected, the resurrection bodies of the righteous.

LIKE A GRAIN OF WHEAT

First Corinthians chapter fifteen deals with this subject of the resurrection body in verses 35–38:

> But someone will say, "How are the dead raised up? And with what body do they come?" Foolish one, what you sow is not made alive unless it dies. And what you sow, you do not sow that body that shall be, but mere grain – perhaps wheat or some other grain. But God gives it a body as He pleases, and to each seed its own body.

Paul is drawing an analogy between two things: a grain of wheat planted in the earth and a believer's body buried in the earth. He is pointing out that there is a correspondence or analogy between what happens to a grain of wheat planted in the ground and to the buried body of a believer.

In the closing chapter of *Foundational Truths For Christian Living*, entitled "Resurrection of the Dead," I have worked out the lessons to be learned from this analogy:

Here Paul uses the analogy of a grain of wheat planted in the ground to illustrate the relationship between the body that is buried and the body that is raised up in resurrection. Out of this analogy there emerge three facts which may be applied to the resurrection of the body:

1. There is direct continuity between the seed that is planted in the ground and the plant that later grows up out of the ground from that seed. The basic material of the original seed is still contained in the plant that grows up out of it.

2. The plant that grows up out of the original seed undergoes, in that process, certain definite and obvious changes. The outward form and appearance of the new plant is different from that of the original seed.

3. The nature of the original seed determines the nature of the plant that grows up out of it. Each kind of seed can produce only the kind of plant that is appropriate to it. A wheat seed can produce only a stalk of wheat; a barley seed can produce only a stalk of barley.

Let us now apply these three facts taken from the analogy of a seed to the nature of the body that is to be resurrected.

1. There is direct continuity between the body that is buried and the body that is resurrected.
2. The body that is resurrected undergoes, in that process, certain definite and obvious changes. The outward form and appearance of the new, resurrected body are different from those of the original body that was buried.
3. The nature of the body that is buried determines the nature of the body that is resurrected. There will be a direct logical and causal connection between the condition of the believer in his present earthly existence and the nature of his [resurrected] body.

pages 458–59

THE RESURRECTION BODY

Then Paul continues in 1 Corinthians on the same theme of the nature of the resurrection body:

> All flesh is not the same flesh, but there is one kind of flesh of men, another flesh of animals, another of fish, and another of birds. There are also celestial bodies and terrestrial bodies; but the glory of the celestial is one, and the glory of the terrestrial is another. There is one glory of the sun, another glory of the moon, and another glory of the stars; for one star differs from another star in glory. So also is the resurrection of the dead.
> 1 Corinthians 15:39–42

Paul makes a number of different points there. First, he points out that even here on earth there are various different kinds of bodies. Bodies of birds, men, fish, beasts, and so on. Then he points out that beyond the earthly realm, in the heavenly realm, there are other kinds of bodies that are very different in kind from the bodies that we are familiar with on earth. He goes on to point out that among these heavenly bodies there are differences in appearance and in glory. The sun differs from the moon. The stars differ from both the sun and moon and from one another, and he applies this to resurrection bodies. He says, "So also is the resurrection of the dead." So the kind of body we have here on earth is one kind, but the kind of body we are going to be resurrected with is a different kind of body, suited to the heavenly regions, which will be our new home.

When a man is put out in space, into the heavenly regions, in a capsule, he has to take earth's atmosphere and conditions with him. His body is not suited to the heavenly regions. It is still an earthly kind of body. But when we each get our new resurrection body, it will not be limited to earth's surface and earth's atmosphere. Then, among the bodies that are given to believers in resurrection, there will be differences in glory, just as there are between the various stars; and the differences in glory will be related to the faithfulness of service of each believer here on earth. So there will be a glory appropriate to the faithfulness of the service of each believer which will be manifested forever in his resurrection body.

Daniel 12:1 also offers a clear prediction of the resurrection: "At that time Michael shall stand up, The great prince who stand watch over the sons of your people...." The "sons of your people" are the Jewish people. And whenever the focus is on Michael in heaven, we know that the Jewish people are center stage on earth.

And there shall be a time of trouble,
Such as never was since there was a nation,
Even to that time.

verse 1

The "time of trouble" is what we call the great tribulation, which will be associated in some way with the resurrection.

And at that time your people shall be delivered,
Every one who is found written in the book.

verse 1

Only those whose names are written in the book (the Book of Life – Revelation 20:12) will be resurrected.

And many of those who sleep in the dust of the earth
    shall awake,
Some to everlasting life,
Some to shame and everlasting contempt.
Those who are wise shall shine
Like the brightness of the firmament,
And those who turn many to righteousness
Like the stars forever and ever.

verses 2–3

That is what Paul is referring to when he says, "For one star differs from another star in glory. So also is the resurrection of the dead." Every one of us will have glory, but those who have turned many to righteousness will shine as the stars forever and ever. One thing we need to bear in mind is God is a Rewarder. We do not work for rewards, but there is a reward. We should not be working for the sake of what we will get, but what we get will be in exact proportion to our faithfulness in this life.

Now we come to five changes that will take place at resurrection. There are certain principles in the Bible associated with numbers. Two is the number of witness, seven is the number of the Holy Spirit, five is the number of things that are visible, that are sensibly perceptible (we have five senses). And so there are

111

five visible, perceptible changes that will take place in our bodies at the resurrection:

> So also is the resurrection of the dead. The body is sown in corruption, it is raised in incorruption. It is sown in dishonor, it is raised in glory. It is sown in weakness, it is raised in power. It is sown a natural body, it is raised a spiritual body. There is a natural body, and there is a spiritual body.
>
> 1 Corinthians 15:42–44

The word translated "natural" in the English version is derived directly from the Greek word for "soul." The most literal translation is "soulish." There is a soulish body and there is a spiritual body. Let me point out one other difference between the natural body that is buried and the resurrection body that will come up out of it, from 1 Corinthians 15:53: "For this corruptible [perishable] must put on incorruption [imperishable], and this mortal must put on immortality."

If we examine all those verses from 1 Corinthians 15 together, we find five specific changes that will take place between the body that is buried and the body that is raised:

1. *From corruptible* (or perishable) *to incorruptible* (or imperishable). Our natural body is subject to corruption – or liable to perish. It is subject to sickness, pain, disease, old age, and decay. Our teeth wear out, our hair falls out, and our skin begins to wrinkle. These are accepted as natural in this earthly body, but it will be quite different in the resurrection body.

2. *From mortal to immortal.* "Mortal" means being subject to death. "Immortal" means not being subject to death. We all know that this present body is subject to death, but the

resurrection body will not be subject to death. It will be immortal.

3. *From dishonor to glory*. We need to understand that the body that we have now is the result of sin. It was not the body that God originally equipped Adam with. It carries on it the marks of man's sin. In a certain sense, it reminds us of our own dishonor. But the resurrection body will be a body of glory. It will no longer remind us of the consequences of our sin.

4. *From weakness to power*. The body that is buried is a weak body. Whenever I attend a funeral, I always think about how weak man is. Death is the ultimate expression of weakness. He may have been a man of great strength or great intelligence or ability, but one day his inherent weakness is made manifest by the fact that he has succumbed to death. The body that is raised, however, will be a body of power.

5. *From natural* (or soulish) *to spiritual*. There is a natural body and there is a spiritual body. The English translation is misleading. The word that is translated *natural* is directly derived from the Greek word for *soul*. It is sown a *soulish* body, it is raised a spiritual body. In various other languages, there is a word for "soulish" (Dutch, German, Scandinavian languages, for instance), but we do not have a word for it. However, I will use the word *soulish* as it is more descriptive.

Most people have not discovered what the difference is between a soulish body and a spiritual body. In order to do this, you have to understand the nature of the natural body. In Psalm 103 when David wanted to praise the Lord, his spirit was ready, but his soul was not prepared. And he could not praise the Lord until he got the cooperation of his soul. So he said, "Bless the

Lord, O my soul." Basically he was saying, "Come on, soul, wake up! Do something!" But it was his spirit that was working on his body through his soul. That describes a *soulish* body.

But in a spiritual body, which most people have never yet seen, the spirit directly controls the body. We have an example of this in Ezekiel. This is the vision that started Ezekiel off as a prophet – a vision of four living creatures.

> They had the likeness of a man. Each one had four faces, and each one had four wings. Their legs were straight, and the soles of their feet were like the soles of calves' feet. They sparkled like the color of burnished bronze.... Thus were their faces. Their wings stretched upward; two wings of each one touched one another, and two covered their bodies. And each one went straight forward; they went wherever the spirit wanted to go, and they did not turn when they went.
>
> Ezekiel 1:5–7, 11:12

These living creatures had spiritual bodies. They did not have to work through the soul. Where each one's spirit wanted to go, they went: "Wherever the spirit wanted to go, they went, because there the spirit went..." (verse 20).

In the resurrection we too will have spiritual bodies, so that we will not have to work through the soul to get the body to do things. The body will respond directly to the spirit. If you think of all the things that your spirit would like to do and your soul is too lazy to do, you will realize what a blessing it will be to have a spiritual body.

This is not easy to explain or understand, but one of the things that is stated in the Scripture is that "the life [or soul] of all flesh is in the blood" (Leviticus 17:11, NAS). Our natural body is a body that contains blood. My personal opinion is that the resurrection body will contain flesh and bones, but no blood.

Beyond that, it will be a body in which the *spirit* directs and controls – and not the soul. Man will be directed from above by his ongoing contact with God. He will not be under the impulses and influences of the soul, as he is in the present body.

WE SHALL BE LIKE HIM

Beloved, now we are children of God; and it has not yet been revealed what we shall be, but we know that when He is revealed, we shall be like Him, for we shall see Him as He is.

1 John 3:2

Already we are the children of God by that inward life that we have: "Christ in us the hope of glory." But that is not yet fully manifest in our external person. That will only happen when Jesus comes and is manifested in His glory. Then we will be like Him. We will receive a body like His. We shall be like Him because we shall see Him as He is. There will be a revelation of the resurrected, glorified Christ to the believers who are waiting for Him that will be transforming in its power. It will transform those mortal bodies into immortal bodies, those weak bodies into strong bodies, those bodies of humiliation into bodies of glory, those corruptible bodies into incorruptible bodies.

Finally, it will be a body of the same order as that of Jesus when He was resurrected:

For our citizenship is in heaven, from which we also eagerly wait for the Savior, the Lord Jesus Christ, who will transform our lowly [vile] body that it may be conformed to His glorious body, according to the working by which He is able even to subdue all things to Himself.

Philippians 3:20–21

Notice that these words are only true of those who are expecting the Lord Jesus to return. Paul speaks about our lowly, vile body but the Greek actually says, "The body of our humiliation." Our bodies have borne the humiliation of the consequences of our sin. We live in a body that continually reminds us of our weakness and limitations. It reminds us that things are not the way that God originally planned they should be. And because of the humiliation, we are reminded of our sin. No matter how wealthy or beautiful a person might be, their body always reminds them of that humiliation: it perspires, it has to eliminate waste, and it is subject to sickness. But thanks be to God, there is this promise that if we are looking for Jesus Christ, when He appears – when we actually see Him – we will be transformed into the likeness of the body of His glory. We will share His glory even in our physical body. And Paul says, and take these words to heart, "... according to the working by which He [Jesus] is able even to subdue all things to Himself."

Do you believe that? Do you believe that Jesus can subdue all things to Himself? Even these weak, corruptible, frail bodies of ours will be subdued and brought into the likeness of His glorious body.

16

JUDGMENT OF BELIEVERS

The next main event that will follow the resurrection of believers is the judgment of believers. That phrase may surprise some of you. You may wonder if there really will be a judgment of believers. Yes, indeed there will! The Scriptures are very clear:

> For it is time for judgment to begin with the family of God; and if it begins with us, what will the outcome be for those who do not obey the gospel of God? And,
>   "If it is hard for the righteous to be saved,
>   What will become of the ungodly and the sinner?"
>   1 Peter 4:17–18, NIV

Judgment begins with the family of God. Then Peter goes on to say that it begins with us, the Christians. You may think, "Why do Christians get resurrected first and then have to face judgment?" The answer is that we are going to answer to God at the resurrection judgment for the things we have done in our body. It is also according to God's scheme of things that, because we are going to answer for what we did in our body, we are going to appear in our body. This is clearly indicated in many passages of Scripture.

THE JUDGMENT SEAT OF CHRIST

The place where the judgment of believers will take place is called, in the New Testament, the judgment seat (or *bema*) of Christ. *Bema* is a Greek word that was common in the culture of that time. It was normally used for the seat on which a Roman magistrate or ruler sat to try a case. When Jesus stood before Pontius Pilate it says that Pilate was sitting on the judgment seat (*bema*) (Matthew 27:19).

> You, then, why do you judge your brother? Or why do you look down on your brother? For we will all stand before God's judgment seat [*bema*]. It is written:
>
> "'As surely as I live,' says the Lord,
>
> 'every knee will bow before me;
>
> every tongue will confess to God.'"
>
> So then, each of us will give an account of himself to God.
>
> Romans 14:10–12, NIV

We are all going to stand before that judgment seat on which Christ will sit as the Judge. We will be receiving what is due to us for the things done while in the body, and, because the judgment is for things done while in the body, we will appear in the body. Paul makes this clear in 2 Corinthians 5:10: "For we must all appear before the judgment seat of Christ, that each one may receive the things done in the body, according to what he has done, whether good or bad."

Notice Paul leaves room only for two kinds of conduct: good or bad. In the spiritual realm there is no neutrality – what we do is either good or it is bad. There is nothing in between. It is either done in obedience and for the glory of God or it is not good. However, it is most important to understand that this judgment of believers will not be a judgment that will result in condemnation. For the true believer in Christ, condemnation is past. In John 5:24 Jesus gives us this assurance: "I tell you the truth, whoever hears my word and believes him who sent me has eternal life and will not be condemned; he has crossed over from death to life" (NIV).

So, whoever hears the Word of God and believes in Jesus *will not be condemned.* He has already crossed over from death to life: "There is therefore now no condemnation to those who are in Christ Jesus" (Romans 8:1).

TO ASSESS SERVICE AND ALLOT REWARDS

If we are in Christ Jesus, we will face a judgment to assess our service and to allot our rewards. In 1 Corinthians 3:11–15 Paul gives us a picture of this judgment of believers:

> For no other foundation can anyone lay than that which is laid, which is Jesus Christ. Now if anyone builds on this foundation with gold, silver, precious stones, wood, hay, straw, each one's work will become clear; for the Day will declare it, because it will be revealed by fire; and the fire will test each one's work, of what sort it is. If anyone's work which he has built on it endures, he will receive a reward. If anyone's work is burned, he will suffer loss; but he himself will be saved, yet so as through fire.

We are speaking here about a person who has built his life on the only foundation acceptable to God, which is the righteousness of Jesus Christ. He will never come into condemnation because his righteousness is the righteousness of Christ. What is being judged here is not the person's soul but his work. This passage speaks about what he has built on that foundation, and it speaks about the quality of his work. So, this is a judgment of work or service, but not a judgment for condemnation.

As we look at the principles upon which work or service is assessed, we notice certain very important details. First, God is more interested in *quality* than *quantity*. The things that are burned up are all things that we can easily assemble in large quantities: wood, hay or straw. But the problem is, they all perish in the fire. The things that will stand the test of fire are things that are difficult to produce in large quantities: gold, silver and precious stones. So it is much more important to concentrate on the quality of what we produce rather than the quantity. It is clear that some ministers and servants of the Lord who amassed great quantities as a result of their service will have the bitter experience of seeing it all perish in the fire of Christ's final judgment and assessment of their work.

If we are to escape this, what should be our aim? I suggest there are three elements we should keep in mind if our service (what we build) is to stand the test of fire. The three things are: *motives, obedience* and *power.*

1. *What are our motives in service?* Are we motivated by selfish ambition, the desire to appear successful before men – to build the biggest church, to call in the largest amount of money, to preach the most famous sermon? Or is it our sincere desire to do that which will glorify God and perhaps remain almost unnoticed and insignificant?

2. *Are we obedient in serving God* according to His Word (His commandments and His principles) or are we building on human theories or our own ideas – theologies that do not accord with the truth of Scripture? We are going to be tested in points of obedience.

3. ***Are we serving God in the power of the Holy Spirit*** or simply in our own fleshly willpower? It is my personal conviction that whatever is done in the flesh will perish like the flesh. Only that which is done in the fire of the Holy Spirit will stand the test of the fire of judgment.

In Matthew 25, Jesus tells a parable of three servants, each of whom received a different number of talents – one received five talents, one received two and one received one. The one who received five gained five more. The one who received two gained two more. Each had a hundred percent gain, and it would appear that each was equally approved by his lord. The words of approval are the same in each case. In other words, it is not so much the quantity we start with, but the *faithfulness* with which we employ what has been allotted to us.

The first two servants were rewarded, but the third, who did nothing whatever with his talent but bury it in the earth, was rejected. He was motivated by fear, not faith. God requires faithfulness but, on the other hand, fear and laziness will bring God's judgment. I would suggest to you that sometime you read the Bible through and see what it has to say about laziness. It never has one good word to say about it. It is far more condemnatory of laziness, for instance, than it is of drunkenness.

In Luke 19, there's another parable about servants who each received the same amount, one pound, but their gains were different. One gained ten pounds, one gained five pounds, and, again, one did nothing with his pound and was rejected. The one who gained ten pounds was rewarded with authority over ten cities. The one who gained five pounds was given authority over five cities.

There are two principles that emerge. First, God looks primarily for faithfulness rather than for ability. It is not the actual gross gain, but the percentage of gain. Each servant that gained a hundred percent increase was equally approved.

The second principle is that reward for faithful service in this life is increased responsibility and opportunities of service in eternity. The greatest thing that anyone could ever do is to serve the true and living God. If we serve Him faithfully in this life, our reward will be greater opportunities of service in the resurrected life.

17

RESURRECTION AND
JUDGMENT
OF UNBELIEVERS

Now we will examine the opposite side of the coin – the resurrection and judgment of the unbelievers. There are two main ways that we can distinguish between these two judgments in Scripture – the judgment of believers before the judgment seat of Christ and the judgment of unbelievers. One is a difference of place; the other is a difference of time.

JUDGMENT	PLACE	TIME
Judgment of Believers	The Judgment Seat of Christ	Before the setting up of Christ's millennial kingdom
Judgment of Unbelievers	The Great White Throne	At the close of the millennial kingdom

THE JUDGMENT OF UNBELIEVERS
The description of the judgment of unbelievers – those who were not resurrected in the resurrection of the righteous – is found in

the book of Revelation. John the revelator paints a vivid picture of what this final and great judgment will be like:

> Then I saw a great white throne and Him who sat on it, from whose face the earth and heaven fled away. And there was found no place for them. [Think of how terrible it will be to appear before the One from whom earth and heaven have to flee when He is in His majesty and in His wrath against sinners.] And I saw the dead, small and great, standing before God, and books were opened. And another book was opened, which is the Book of Life. And the dead were judged according to their works, by the things which were written in the books. The sea gave up the dead who were in it, and Death and Hades delivered up the dead who were in them. And they were judged, each one according to his works. Then Death and Hades were cast into the lake of fire. This is the second death. And anyone not found written in the Book of Life was cast into the lake of fire.
>
> Revelation 20:11–15

These people now resurrected, even after resurrection, are still called "the dead." John said, "I saw the dead, small and great, standing before God." Even after resurrection they were still dead. Their bodies had been restored to them, but they were still dead. They were dead in trespasses and sins, alienated and cut off from the life of God, resurrected in their bodies to receive judgment for what they had done in their bodies.

Note also that there are universal records kept of everything that every one of us has ever done. It is all recorded. Note also that there is universal accountability. Every one of us will be required to answer for what we have done. That word *account-ability* is most unacceptable in the ears of modern culture. There are many different religions and philosophies today of which the supreme objective is to declare to man that he is not really accountable to anybody but himself. I want to serve notice to you, that is a lie! Man is accountable to his Creator, who will one day be his Judge. All of us are accountable.

THOSE EXEMPT: THE OVERCOMERS

The final point that I wish to make here is that there is only one way of escape: through the Book of Life. Everyone whose name was not written in the Book of Life was thrown into the lake of fire. This is irrevocable, eternal banishment from the presence of Almighty God, but it is not a cessation of consciousness. Once we attain consciousness, it continues forever and ever.

What kind of person, has his name written in the Book of Life? Obviously, this is a vital question for each one of us. In the next chapter of Revelation, John goes on to describe the kind of person whose name is written in the Book of Life, and also the kind of person who will be thrown into the lake of fire:

> He who overcomes shall inherit all things [all the glories of heaven], and I will be his God and he shall be My son. But the cowardly, unbelieving, abominable, murderers, sexually immoral, sorcerers, idolaters, and all liars shall have their part in the lake which burns with fire and brimstone, which is the second death.
>
> Revelation 21:7–8

So the primary requirement for those whose names are written in the Book of Life is to *overcome*. This means to not be defeated by sin and by the world or by ungodliness and by Satan. "He who overcomes shall inherit all things, and I will be his God and he will be My son."

The alternative is stated in verse eight – those kinds of persons who will end in the lake of fire. You might agree that immoral persons, murderers, sorcerers and liars will be there, but notice that the first two in the list are the *cowardly* and *unbelieving*. Those are the first two categories of people who are lost. A person can get to heaven without theology, but I doubt whether a person will ever get to heaven without courage.

John addresses this also in his first epistle:

> For whatever is born of God overcomes the world. And this is the victory that has overcome the world – our faith. Who is he who overcomes the world, but he who believes that Jesus is the Son of God?
>
> 1 John 5:4–5

The requirement, then, is to be born of God – through faith. We are required to believe that Jesus is the Son of God. He who believes that Jesus is the Son of God and is born again through that faith, has the faith to overcome the world. That overcoming faith will cause him to inherit all things. God will be his God, and he will be the son of God.

JESUS: THE WATERSHED OF HUMAN SOULS

As we contemplate the scene of final judgment before the great white throne, certain thoughts always come to me. I would like to share one of them with you. Some years ago, I was in the state of Colorado, in the Rocky Mountains, and someone pointed a little west of where we were and said, "That ridge there is the watershed of the continental United States." They went on to explain that rain that fell on one side went down into the Pacific area, and the rain that fell on the other side ultimately flowed down into the Gulf of Mexico. Even though there might only be the difference of just one or two inches between the raindrops that fell, their ultimate destination was thousands of miles apart.

As I was picturing that in my mind, I said to myself, *Jesus is the watershed of human souls.* Their destiny in eternity is determined by which side of Jesus they are on. Two souls can be so close together – even husband and wife or parent and child or brother and sister – yet one is on the one side of Jesus (having received Him and believed in Him), and the other is on the other side (not having believed and not having received). Though they are so close in this life, their ultimate destiny is an immeasurable distance apart. One will end in the eternal glory of heaven; the other will end in the lake of fire, the place of eternal judgment and punishment for unbelievers. That tiny difference of two inches in where a raindrop falls in the Rockies determines its ultimate destination.

So it is with you and me: just a tiny difference in this life – on one side of Jesus or the other – will determine our eternal destiny. On which side of Jesus are you?

This picture of the two raindrops impresses upon me the responsibility that preachers have to present the full truth of the gospel. Paul said to the elders in Ephesus:

> I did not shrink from declaring to you anything that was profitable, and teaching you publicly and from house to house, solemnly testifying to both Jews and Greeks of repentance toward God and faith in our Lord Jesus Christ.... Therefore I testify to you this day, that I am innocent of the blood of all men. For I did not shrink from declaring to you the whole purpose of God.
>
> Acts 20:20–21, 26–27, NAS

Twice Paul said that he did not shrink from telling the whole truth – everything that God said they needed to know. But why did he use the words, "I did not shrink"? I think it is because there is a kind of pressure against the preacher who tells the whole truth. The devil does not mind someone preaching sermons, as long as they do not contain the vital truths. But there are tremendous pressures against the man who will stand up and declare the whole truth. They may be social or financial pressures affecting his entire destiny. How many preachers among us today could say, like Paul, "I did not shrink from declaring to you the whole purpose of God"?

What are the decisive requirements upon which salvation depends? Paul states them very simply: repentance toward God and faith in Jesus Christ. That and that alone can save us from that awful destination – the lake of fire – and take us into eternal glory with Jesus.

Remember, *no one will drift into heaven.* It has to be your first priority. You have to belong totally and unreservedly to Jesus Christ. That is not something terrible. It is something wonderful. But you have to be clear in your own mind that is what it takes. So make a decision. Make an unreserved commitment to Jesus. He is a wonderful companion – the best friend you could ever want.

I have had wonderful friends through the years and two wonderful wives, each much better than I ever deserved. But no one compares with Jesus. He is in a class by Himself. He is perfect: so loving and so faithful, so patient and understanding. He understands your weaknesses, your temptations, and all that you are going through. If you will commit yourself to Him, you have His promise: "I will never leave you nor forsake you."

If you are not sure that you belong unreservedly to Jesus but you want to commit yourself to Him without reservation, here is a prayer that you can say:

Lord Jesus Christ, I believe that you are the Son of God and the only way to God. I believe that You died on the cross for my sins, You were buried, and You rose again the third day. And now all authority in heaven and on earth is given to You because of what You did for me on the cross when You bore my sins and paid my penalty. On that basis, I ask You now to forgive all my sins and I commit my life to You now that You may be my Lord and my Savior, and that I may belong to You now and throughout eternity. Lord Jesus, because of Your mercy and because of Your promises, I believe that You now receive me and I give You thanks. In Jesus' Name.

18

How to Face Death

We have seen from previous chapters that our destiny will depend on one thing, our personal relationship to Jesus Christ. He is the watershed of human souls. Faith in Jesus assures us of pardon, peace and eternal life. On the other hand, unbelief will just as surely bring upon us judgment and rejection by God.

Now let's make a very personal and practical application of these truths. Before I start, let me remind you once more that one of the appointments you are not going to miss is the one I am addressing now. I suggest to you that if you are to face death with peace, confidence and calm assurance, there are four main steps you are going to need to take.

Face It!

First, you have to face it. Face the fact that *you* are going to die, *I* am going to die, *each one* of us is going to die. As a minister, I'm often amazed at how few people are prepared for death. People can go through life knowing full well that they are going to die and never make adequate preparation for that sure event. It is not morbid to face the fact that you are going to die, it is simply realistic. On the other hand, it is very unrealistic to live out your life without making preparation for what inevitably will comes at the end.

Consider what Paul says about himself in Philippians 1:21: "For to me, to live is Christ, and to die is gain."

Paul was not afraid of dying. He had faced the realities of sin, of judgment and of God's requirements in his life, and because he had been willing to face them and to face the issue of death, he had passed into a relationship with God where there was no more fear. There was only a keen desire to be released from the bondage of this fleshly life and to enter into the fullness of God's presence. Every one of us who will do the same as Paul did can have this same calm assurance. We can say as Paul said, "To live is Christ, but to die is gain." But I want to suggest to you that if you cannot say, "To live is Christ," then you cannot say, "To die is gain." Get related to God through Jesus Christ in such a way that there is no more condemnation, no more fear and no more uncertainty.

ACCEPT GOD'S OFFER

Facing death leads to the second step: accept God's offer of pardon, peace, and eternal life. Then you can say with Paul: "Therefore, having been justified by faith, we have peace with God through our Lord Jesus Christ" (Romans 5:1).

In order to be justified we must put our faith in the sacrificial death of Jesus Christ, acknowledging that He has borne the guilt of our sin. You remember how I described what it is to be justified? Justified is "just-as-if-I'd never sinned," because I have a righteousness imputed to me that has never known sin – the righteousness of Jesus Christ. In that righteousness I can face God, death and eternity without a tremor or a fear.

And this is the testimony: that God has given us eternal life, and this life is in His Son. He who has the Son has the life; he who does not have the Son of God does not have life. These things I have written to you who believe in the name of the Son of God, that you may know that you have eternal life.

1 John 5:11–13

God has given a testimony to the entire human race, that He has offered us eternal life. This life is in the person of His Son, Jesus Christ. If we receive Jesus Christ, in Him we have received eternal life. Notice, it is in the present tense: "He who has the Son, has the life." It is not something that is going to happen after death, but something that happens now in this time/space world. If you leave it until after death, you will have left it too late. You need to settle that issue *now*! He who has the Son has life!

Notice, too, what John says in verse 13: "These things I have written to you who believe in the name of the Son of God, that you may know that you have eternal life." It is not merely that we believe, but that through believing we can come to know. You may say, "I believe in Jesus," but I want to ask you, "Do you know?" The end purpose of believing is knowing, and those of us who *believe* the way God requires us to believe in Jesus Christ also *know* that we have eternal life. We have it now; we are not waiting for it after death. We know that when death comes, it cannot touch or destroy the eternal life that we already have in Jesus Christ.

Dedicate Yourself to Christ's Service

The third step is to dedicate yourself here and now to Christ's service in this world. In chapter 16, I pointed out that we all are going to stand as believers before the judgment seat of Christ to receive the things done in our bodies, whether good or bad

(2 Corinthians 5:10). I reminded you that there are only two categories for what we do in this life. They are either good or they are bad. Anything that is not positively good is positively bad. So, we have to dedicate ourselves to Christ in such a way that what we do is good and that it is acceptable to God.

In this connection, I pointed out that we need to check ourselves in three areas: motives, obedience and power. What are our motives? Are they self-seeking? Are we seeking our own ambition, our own pleasure, our own self-satisfaction or glory? Or are we sincerely motivated by the desire for God's glory? God is going to sift our motives one day.

Second, are we serving God on His terms, or on ours? Are we obedient to the clear statements and requirements of Scripture, or are we trying to fashion some kind of new religion of our own that suits us better than the requirements of Scripture? We are going to be sifted on the question of obedience.

Third, are we serving God in our own power or in His power? Have we allowed the Holy Spirit to come in and take complete control of us, to motivate and empower us. Are we serving God in a way that is acceptable to Him?

Let God Wean You from the Things of Time

The fourth step takes a little more explaining, but it is very important. It is to let God wean you from the things of time. I will introduce it with one of my favorite passages:

> The voice said, "Cry out!"
> And he [the prophet] said, "What shall I cry?"
>
> "All flesh is grass,
> And all its loveliness is like the flower of the field.
> The grass withers, the flower fades,

Because the breath [or Spirit] of the Lord blows
    upon it;
Surely the people are grass.
The grass withers, the flower fades,
But the word of our God stands forever."

Isaiah 40:6–8

How true a picture of life that is! We are surrounded by things that are beautiful and by people we love. There is so much to love and to appreciate, and yet everything that we see is grass – ourselves included. It blossoms and flourishes in the morning and perishes by nightfall.

The Bible tells us that the grass withers and fades because the Spirit (or the breath) of the Lord blows upon it. I used to wonder about that, and then one day God showed me this truth. God gives loveliness in the temporal world, and then He causes it to wither. Why? Because He wants us to know about loveliness. He wants us to know the loveliness that He is capable of producing, but He never wants us to be permanently at home in this world. So He arouses our sense of loveliness, our appreciation of beauty in all that is good, and then He causes the temporary loveliness of this world to wither. He does this so that we may set our hearts on the loveliness that is beyond this world and in the next. This is how God weans us from the things of time.

The Bible is very realistic. It says that: "If only for this life we have hope in Christ, we are to be pitied more than all men" (1 Corinthians 15:19, NIV). Does your faith in Christ extend into eternity? If not, your religion is a pitiful fantasy. If our hope in Christ is genuine, it does not cease with this life. It gets brighter and brighter throughout eternity.

This hope produces a lifestyle that is different. Paul admonishes us in Colossians 3:1–4:

Since, then, you have been raised with Christ, set your hearts on things above, where Christ is seated at the right hand of God. Set your minds on things above, not on earthly things. For you died, and your life is now hidden with Christ in God. When Christ, who is your life, appears, then you also will appear with him in glory.

NIV

Notice, your hearts and your minds – your affections and the things you think about – are to be set on the things above. The ultimate reward of the believer is beyond the things of time. That is when our true life, which is Christ, will be manifested in its glory and fullness. That still lies ahead, beyond the grave.

Death does not need to be an accident, something that comes untimely or too soon, as something that you are not prepared for. If you are moving in the purposes of God, you can come to death like a sheaf that is ripe in its season, and God will gather you in at the appointed time. This is the promise of Job 5:26: "You will come to the grave in full vigor, like sheaves gathered in season" (NIV).

At the end of World War II Lydia and I were living north of Jerusalem in Ramallah, which was then a quiet, Christian Arab town. In that town there was an Arab woman, a believer, who died. My first wife, Lydia, asked the woman's grandson, "What did she die of?" The grandson thought for a moment and then answered, "She didn't die of anything. She was ripe, that's all."

What a beautiful answer! How are you going to die? Ripe or unripe? Remember one thing, you do not have to die sick. There are very few believers in the Bible of whom it is recorded that they died sick. If you live the Bible way, you die, not because you are sick, but because you are ripe.

19

How to Face the Death of a Loved One

I believe there are some things a person can only understand after experiencing them. This was true in my own case. In 1975, the Lord called home my first wife, Lydia. We had had thirty years of happy married life together. We had shared everything – poverty, riches, good times and bad times. We had raised a family of nine adopted girls together, and we had served the Lord together. Sometimes, after we had been ministering together in a service or a conference, people would come up to us and say something like, "You two work together just like one person." That was the kind of unity there was between us. When the Lord called Lydia home, it was like a part of me was taken away. It was the most agonizing experience of my life.

I had a wonderful marriage with Lydia, but we were always in the midst of a large, busy family. In my second marriage with Ruth, however, God so arranged things that we spent most of our time together by ourselves. For twenty years, we traveled by ourselves, we prayed by ourselves, we worked by ourselves, and we did so many things together by ourselves. I experienced in my relationship with Ruth a kind of intimacy that I have never known with any other person and that I never expect to know again until I get to heaven.

But again, in December 1998, God called Ruth home, too. At the interment service for Ruth in the German colony in Jerusalem, I was standing in front of the open grave looking down on her casket before they filled the earth in, and I felt prompted to cry out, "Father, I trust You. I thank You that You are always kind. You are always kind and loving and just. You never make a mistake. What You do is always the best." It was one of the hardest things I have ever done in my life, and it was also one of the best.

Since then, I began to observe others, and when bereaved men and women were attracted to me, I was able to comfort them in a way that I had not been able to do before. I came to realize how few people are prepared for the death of a loved one. A man and a woman can live together for thirty or forty or fifty years and yet not be prepared when God calls one of them home. Surely, that is unrealistic because one will die before the other. Very seldom does a married couple go together. Or it may happen that God may take a brother, a sister, or some other loved relative. And remember, parents, that God takes children home, too. They do not all grow up to full age and maturity. There are caskets of all sizes because people of all ages die. I am not being morbid when I say this, but realistic. I discovered, however, that we can face the death of a loved one in victory. It can prove yet another evidence of God's love and faithfulness.

On the basis of my experiences, I want to offer you some counsel on what you should do if and when you are faced with this situation.

1. *Trust God's love and wisdom.* There is a beautiful example

of this in the story of Job. Job's seven sons and three daughters had all been taken by death in a moment – in a single disaster. But this is what Job said, "The Lord gave, and the Lord has taken away; blessed be the name of the Lord" (Job 1:21). I do not believe that was said in resignation; I believe that was said in trust. If you can trust the Lord to give, can you not trust the Lord to take away? Can you not trust His wisdom? Doesn't God know the right way and right time to take each one of His children? I believe He does.

2. *Yield the loved one to God.* That is not easy. I remember about an hour after Lydia died, I said to the Lord, "I won't ask for her back. She was yours before she was mine." When I said that, it was like something was pulled out of my heart, and it made room for the hand of God to move in and to begin healing the wound. But as long as I was holding on to her with my soulish desire, God could not really move on my behalf. So my second piece of counsel is: yield up the loved one.

When Ruth passed away, I said to God, "Father, I trust You." I realize now, looking back, that at that point I had come to a fork in the highway of my life. I could have gone one or the other of two ways. I could have become bitter and complained and cried out to God, "Why did You take Ruth? You know how much I needed her. You were the One who joined us together." I could have blamed God. But I did not do that. I decided to trust God and believe that He did what was best both for Ruth and for me.

3. *Reaffirm your faith.* It may sound strange for a preacher to say this, but when God took both of my wives I had to ask myself each time, "Do I really believe what I have been preaching all these years? Do I really believe there will be a resurrection? Do I really believe that I will see them again?" For a little while it was hard for me to answer. Then I said, "I do believe! I do

believe! There will be a resurrection! We will meet again! God is faithful! The Bible is to be trusted!" I have not put my faith in something that is unreal and insubstantial, but I have put my faith in something that will stand every test – the faithfulness of God, the love of God, and the truth of Scripture. When you are faced with this kind of situation, reaffirm your faith. Every time you do it, your faith will be strengthened, and you will have greater victory in your soul.

4. ***Don't try to be stoical.*** Don't bottle up your feelings! Stoicism is a pagan philosophy that originated in Greece. The Stoic was the one who would not let anything hurt him. He was so in control of everything that he never laughed or cried. In fact, he never showed his emotions. That has nothing to do with the Christian faith. God knows we are human beings. The Scripture says He knows what we are made of. He knows our feelings and our thoughts. God knows that you are hurting and that you experience grief, and He is not angry with you for that.

I have always been impressed with the fact that in the history of Israel, after their redemption from Egypt, they lost their two great leaders – Moses and Aaron (see Deuteronomy 34:8–12 and Numbers 20:23–29). In each case, God permitted Israel thirty days of mourning for their leaders. God knew that they could not just get up and go on as though nothing had happened. God knew that something had been taken out of their lives that they were going to miss, and He said, "Take thirty days and express your feelings – don't bottle it up."

I think also of the testimony of David:

You have turned for me my mourning into dancing;
You have put off my sackcloth and clothed me with
gladness,

To the end that my glory may sing praise to You and
   not be silent.
O Lord, my God, I will give thanks to You forever.

Psalm 30:11–12

The Bible is so honest, so realistic. David did not say that he
did not mourn, he acknowledged that he did mourn. He said, "I
know what mourning is." But he also said that his mourning had
turned into dancing. I do not believe that David would ever have
danced if he had not mourned. There is a dancing that comes
only out of mourning.

In my own personal experience, that actually happened to
me. God literally turned my mourning into dancing, but I had to
mourn first. I had to be honest and realistic. I had to admit that
I was grieving and that it hurt. But God heals that hurt when we
expose it to Him with honesty. If you try to bottle that feeling up,
it will just go inward where it will fester, and one day you might
have some kind of emotional problem. Today I feel that I am a
healthier and stronger person, both mentally and emotionally,
than I was before I went through those experiences with Lydia
and with Ruth.

5. *Lean on your fellow believers.* In 1 Thessalonians 4:18 Paul
challenges us: "Therefore comfort one another with these words."
There are times when we need comfort from our fellow believers.
One thing I will never forget is the love that was shown me by
countless friends and family, as well as church members.

Each time either Lydia and I or Ruth and I took up residence
in a new location, we were careful to make ourselves part of a
local congregation. I believe it is so important for everyone to
be under pastoral care. I thank God for the pastors who stood
by me in these hard times. It is something that will stay with me

for the rest of my life. Also, it made a tremendous impact upon others around me.

I look back and I thank God that I was part of a body – a committed group of believers who shared their lives with each other. Believe me, when your hour of crisis comes you are going to need people to comfort you. It is beautiful that the Scripture calls God, "The God of all comfort" (2 Corinthians 1:3). One main way He comforts us is through our fellow believers. This is beautifully expressed in Ecclesiastes 4:9–10:

Two are better than one,
Because they have a good return for their labor.
For if they fall, the one will lift up his companion.
But woe to him who is alone when he falls,
For he has no one to help him up.

Remember, there is going to be a time when you will need committed believers who will stand by you.

6. *Continue to serve Christ as faithfully as you can*. Do not let anything hold you back from your own personal obligation to the Lord to serve Him and to fulfill the ministry He has given you.

Brethren, I do not count myself to have apprehended; but one thing I do, forgetting those things which are behind and reaching forward to those things which are ahead, I press toward the goal for the prize of the upward call of God in Christ Jesus.

Philippians 3:13–14

One of the secrets of successful Christian living is to be able to forget what lies behind and reach on to what lies ahead. There is a prize ahead! Press toward it!

As I look back on those times of mourning, they have become yet another proof in my own life and experience of God's love and God's faithfulness.

20

WITNESSES TO OUR GENERATION

The knowledge of Christ's resurrection places us under a solemn personal obligation to be witnesses to our generation. This is confirmed in the following passage, which is a conversation between Jesus and His disciples after He was resurrected.

ADJUSTED PRIORITIES

> Therefore, when they had come together, they asked Him, saying, "Lord, will You at this time restore the kingdom to Israel?" And He said to them, "It is not for you to know the times or seasons which the Father has put in His own authority. But you shall receive power when the Holy Spirit has come upon you; and you shall be witnesses to Me in Jerusalem, and in all Judea and Samaria, and to the end of the earth."
>
> Acts 1:6–8

Jesus adjusted the priorities of the disciples. They were primarily concerned with the restoration of the earthly kingdom of

Israel. Jesus did not say that it would not happen, but He said the time and the way in which it would be brought about is something that the Father has put under His own authority. Then He said, in essence, "That is not the thing about which I want you to be primarily concerned. You have a personal responsibility, and I want you to be faithful in discharging that responsibility."

The responsibility that Jesus placed upon His disciples was to be His witnesses – witnesses of Him – where they were and then in an ever-extending circle that would not cease until it had reached the end of the earth. But He pointed out that in order to be effective witnesses they needed to experience a supernatural infilling of the Holy Spirit. You see, the resurrection of Christ is something totally supernatural. And we need a supernatural power to bear effective witness to this supernatural event. So Jesus said, in effect, "You're going to be witnesses, but don't go out and start trying to do the job in your own ability and cleverness or even in your own intellectual knowledge of Me and My teaching. Wait until you receive supernatural power which will make your testimony to this supernatural event fully convincing." Then He said, "You will be witnesses to Me in this ever-extending circle of which the center is Jerusalem and the circumference is the end of the earth."

So He adjusted their priorities. He said, "Prophetic insight isn't the first thing. Doctrinal knowledge isn't the first thing. The first thing is to lead such a life that you will be witnesses to Me wherever you go."

CHRISTIANITY: A WAY OF LIFE

It is important that we see that is still true today. Christianity is primarily not a matter of doctrinal or intellectual knowledge or understanding of prophecy. But it is a matter of how we live.

In the book of Acts, the first description given to Christianity is in the phrase "the way." People who were related to the early church saw Christians as people representing not some theory but representing a way of life. And that is what Christianity is primarily today – it is a way of life that makes us witnesses to Jesus and, particularly, to His resurrection.

This is exemplified by the kind of life that the apostles lived as Paul describes it in 1 Corinthians 15:30–31: "And why do we stand in jeopardy [or danger] every hour? I affirm, by the boasting in you which I have in Christ Jesus our Lord, I die daily."

Paul's lifestyle was a "death style." But he never was concerned because he knew that even if he died he would be resurrected. We also need to know that even if we do not lead the same kind of adventurous life as Paul, sooner or later we are going to die. That is one certain fact.

EVIL COMPANY CORRUPTS GOOD HABITS

If you are to be a faithful witness to the resurrection of Jesus, you must be careful about the company you keep. If you associate with the wrong people, they will take your faith away from you. Do not be deceived: "Evil company corrupts good habits" (1 Corinthians 15:33). You must be circumspect in your close fellowship with unbelievers. You can be merciful, you can be gracious, and you can be loving, but you must not let their example dictate your lifestyle because it will destroy your faith. Paul warns us in verse 34: "Awake to righteousness, and do not sin; for some do not have the knowledge of God. I speak this to your shame."

Some Christians do not have the knowledge of God. They really do not know God's plan of salvation. Speaking to such Christians, Paul says, "I speak this to your shame." In effect Paul is saying: "You should know. What have you been doing in church all these years? What have you been listening to?" Then he might have added: "Maybe you have been listening to lies. Maybe you have been listening to false and foolish criticisms of the gospel. Be careful what you listen to." Jesus said, "Take heed what you hear. With the same measure you use, it will be measured to you" (Mark 4:24).

I am very careful about what I open my mind to. Ruth used to say about me, "I have never met anybody who is so careful about what he lets into his mind." Do you know why? Because if I let something into my mind, sooner or later it is going to come out of my mouth. As a messenger of God, I do not want to bring to people anything but the pure, simple, undefiled truth of Scripture.

In another instance, when the apostles decided that they had to appoint a successor to Judas Iscariot, this is how they expressed it:

> Therefore, of these men who have accompanied us all the time that the Lord Jesus went in and out among us, beginning from the baptism of John to that day when He [Jesus] was taken up from us, one of these must become a witness with us of His resurrection.

Acts 1:21–22

The primary function of an apostle was not primarily to be a preacher or a teacher. It was to be a witness together with the other apostles of the resurrection of Jesus. And the essential point of the witness was that Jesus had risen from the dead. "And with great power the apostles gave witness to the resurrection of the Lord Jesus. And great grace was upon them all" (Acts 4:33).

The supernatural power that Jesus had promised them made

their testimony effective. But they were not primarily preaching. They were giving witness to the resurrection of the Lord Jesus. I believe that every person on the face of the earth has a right to know that Jesus rose from the dead. It is our responsibility to tell them. What they do with the knowledge becomes their responsibility. But if they never hear, then we have failed in our responsibility. God requires us to be His witnesses.

There is a difference between being a witness and being a preacher. A preacher unfolds biblical truths. He has to have a special calling to do that. But a witness merely speaks out of personal experience. He relates what has happened in his own experience through God, through Jesus Christ, through the Holy Spirit and through the message of the Gospel. I have heard this definition: to be a witness means to lead a life that can only be explained by the fact that Jesus is alive. That is what God requires of all of us. Whether we are preachers or not is secondary. Whether we understand all prophecies and all doctrines is secondary. But the primary requirement is that we personally be witnesses of the resurrection of Jesus Christ.

I am a Witness

I was educated in Britain between the two world wars. I was privileged to attend two of Britain's most prestigious institutions: Eton College and Cambridge University. I studied Latin from the age of nine and Greek from the age of ten. I obtained many scholarships, and at a very early age I was elected into a Fellowship (resident Professorship) in King's College, Cambridge. I say all that not to boast, but simply to show you that if intellectual education could satisfy the needs of a man's heart, my needs would have been satisfied. But they were not. I was an unfulfilled, searching person.

I studied philosophy because I was searching for the meaning and purpose of life, but philosophy did not provide me with an answer. Academically I was successful, but inwardly I was frustrated. I did not know where to look for an answer.

Then, by an unplanned set of circumstances during World War II, I met some people who really were witnesses. They were humble and not highly educated, but their lives spoke to me of the fact that they knew Jesus personally as being alive today. That created in me a desperate desire to have what they had. I had no doctrinal knowledge and did not understand the message of the Gospel. I only knew that these people had something that I had been looking for all my life.

Eventually, in desperation, in an army barrack room in the middle of the night, I prayed and asked God in the simplest way to give me what those people had. I will thank God forever – He gave it to me! He revealed Jesus to me directly, personally and in an extremely powerful way so that there was no room left in my mind for doubt that Jesus Christ is alive and that I knew Him. From that day to this, I have never been able to doubt that fact.

That revelation of Jesus did for me all that the New Testament declares it will do. It totally, radically and permanently changed me – my character, my attitudes, my ambitions and my purposes in life. It gave me a reason for living that has kept me active and full of life and vigor and with a purpose to pursue until this very day. I want to tell you out of my personal experience: Jesus is alive!

Now in my late eighties, I know that soon I will come to the end of life's journey. I am not afraid at all. I look forward to all the glories in the life to come – and the many people I will meet (and see again!) in Heaven. This theme of victory over death is both real and practical to me, and I trust that you too now have the knowledge that Christ makes available to you also victory over death!

About the Author

Derek Prince (1915–2003) was born in India of British parents. Educated as a scholar of Greek and Latin at Eton College and Cambridge University, England, he held a Fellowship in Ancient and Modern Philosophy at King's College. He also studied several modern languages, including Hebrew and Aramaic, at Cambridge University and the Hebrew University in Jerusalem.

While serving with the British army in World War II, he began to study the Bible and experienced a life-changing encounter with Jesus Christ. Out of this encounter he formed two conclusions: first, that Jesus Christ is alive; second, that the Bible is a true, relevant, up-to-date book. These conclusions altered the whole course of his life, which he then devoted to studying and teaching the Bible.

Derek's main gift of explaining the Bible and its teaching in a clear and simple way has helped build a foundation of faith in millions of lives. His non-denominational, non-sectarian approach has made his teaching equally relevant and helpful to people from all racial and religious backgrounds.

He is the author of over 50 books, 600 audio and 110 video

teachings, many of which have been translated and published in more than 100 languages. His daily radio broadcast is translated into Arabic, Bahass (Indonesia), Chinese (Amoy, Cantonese, Mandarin, Shanghaiese, Swatow), Croatian, German, Malagasy, Mongolian, Russian, Samoan, Spanish and Tongan. The radio program continues to touch lives around the world.

Derek Prince Ministries persists in reaching out to believers in over 140 countries with Derek's teachings, fulfilling the mandate to keep on "until Jesus returns." This is effected through the outreaches of more than 45 Derek Prince offices around the world, including primary work in Australia, Canada, China, France, Germany, the Netherlands, New Zealand, Norway, Russia, South Africa, Switzerland, the United Kingdom and the United States.

For current information about these and other worldwide locations, visit www.derekprince.com.

Books by Derek Prince

Appointment in Jerusalem
At the End of Time*
Authority and Power of God's Word*
Be Perfect
Blessing or Curse: You Can Choose
Bought with Blood
By Grace Alone
Called to Conquer
Choice of a Partner, The
Complete Salvation
Declaring God's Word
Derek Prince – A Biography by Stephen Mansfield
Derek Prince: On Experiencing God's Power
Destiny of Israel and The Church, The
Divine Exchange, The
Doctrine of Baptisms, The*
Does Your Tongue Need Healing?
Entering the Presence of God
Expelling Demons

Orphans, Widows, the Poor and Oppressed
Our Debt to Israel
Pages from My Life's Book
Partners for Life
Philosophy, the Bible and the Supernatural
Power in the Name
Power of the Sacrifice, The
Prayers and Proclamations
Praying for the Government
Promise of Provision, The
Prophetic Guide to the End Times
Protection from Deception
Pulling Down Strongholds
Receiving God's Best
Rediscovering God's Church
Resurrection of the Body*
Rules of Engagement
Secrets of a Prayer Warrior
Self-Study Bible Course (revised and expanded)
Set Apart for God
Shaping History Through Prayer and Fasting
Sharing in Christ'sVictory Over Death
Spiritual Warfare
Surviving the Last Days
Thanksgiving, Praise and Worship
They Shall Expel Demons
Three Most Powerful Words, The
Through Repentance to Faith*
Through the Psalms with Derek Prince
Transmitting God's Power*
Three Messages for Israel

Two Harvests, The

War in Heaven

Where Wisdom Begins

Who is the Holy Spirit?

Will You Intercede?

You Matter to God

You Shall Receive Power

GET THE COMPLETE LAYING THE FOUNDATIONS SERIES*

1. Founded on the Rock (B100)

2. Authority and Power of God's Word (B101)

3. Through Repentance to Faith (B102)

4. Faith and Works (B103)

5. The Doctrine of Baptisms (B104)

6. Immersion in The Spirit (B105)

7. Transmitting God's Power (B106)

8. At the End of Time (B107)

9. Resurrection of the Body (B108)

10. Final Judgment (B109)

Derek Prince Ministries

www.derekprince.com

Derek Prince Ministries Offices Worldwide

DPM – Asia/Pacific
38 Hawdon Street
Sydenham
Christchurch 8023
New Zealand
T: + 64 3 366 4443
E: admin@dpm.co.nz
W: www.dpm.co.nz

DPM – Australia
15 Park Road
Seven Hills
New South Wales 2147
Australia
T: +61 2 9838 7778
E: enquiries@au.derekprince.com
W: www.derekprince.com.au

DPM – Canada
P.O. Box 8354 Halifax
Nova Scotia B3K 5M1
Canada
T: + 1 902 443 9577
E: enquiries.dpm@eastlink.ca
W: www.derekprince.org

DPM – France
B.P. 31, Route d'Oupia
34210 Olonzac
France
T: + 33 468 913872
E: info@derekprince.fr
W: www.derekprince.fr

DPM – Germany
Söldenhofstr. 10
83308 Trostberg
Germany
T: + 49 8621 64146
E: ibl@ibl-dpm.net
W: www.ibl-dpm.net

DPM – Netherlands
Nobelstraat 7–08
7131 PZ Lichtenvoorde
Netherlands
T: + 31 251 255044
E: info@derekprince.nl
W: www.derekprince.nl

DPM – Norway
P.O. Box 129
Lodderfjord
N-5881 Bergen
Norway
T: +47 928 39855
E: sverre@derekprince.no
W: www.derekprince.no

Derek Prince Publications Pte. Ltd.
P.O. Box 2046
Robinson Road Post Office
Singapore 904046
T: + 65 6392 1812
E: dpmchina@singnet.com.sg
W: www.dpmchina.org (English)
   www.ygmweb.org (Chinese)

DPM – South Africa
P.O. Box 33367
Glenstantia
0010 Pretoria
South Africa
T: +27 12 348 9537
E: enquiries@derekprince.co.za
W: www.derekprince.co.za

DPM – Switzerland
Alpenblick 8
CH-8934 Knonau
Switzerland
T: + 41 44 768 25 06
E: dpm-ch@ibl-dpm.net
W: www.ibl-dpm.net

DPM – UK
P.O. Box 393
Hitchin SG5 9EU
United Kingdom
T: + 44 1462 492100
E: enquiries@dpmuk.org
W: www.dpmuk.org

DPM – USA
P.O. Box 19501
Charlotte NC 28219
USA
T: + 1 704 357 3556
E: ContactUs@derekprince.org
W: www.derekprince.org